TWAYNE'S WORLD AUTHORS SERIES

A Survey of the World's Literature

Sylvia E. Bowman, Indiana University

GENERAL EDITOR

GERMANY

Ulrich Weisstein, Indiana University

EDITOR

Hermann Hesse

TWAS 93

TWAYNE'S WORLD AUTHORS SERIES (TWAS)

*The purpose of TWAS is to survey the major writers
—novelists, dramatists, historians, poets, philosophers,
and critics—of the nations of the world. Among the
national literatures covered are those of Australia,
Canada, China, Eastern Europe, France, Germany,
Greece, India, Italy, Japan, Latin America, New Zea-
land, Poland, Russia, Scandinavia, Spain, and the
African nations, as well as Hebrew, Yiddish, and
Latin Classical literatures. This survey is comple-
mented by Twayne's United States Authors Series
and English Authors Series.*

*The intent of each volume in these series is to present
a critical-analytical study of the works of the writer;
to include biographical and historical material that
may be necessary for understanding, appreciation,
and critical appraisal of the writer; and to present all
material in clear, concise English—but not to vitiate
the scholarly content of the work by doing so.*

Hermann Hesse

By GEORGE WALLIS FIELD

Victoria College

TWAYNE PUBLISHERS

A DIVISION OF G. K. HALL & CO., BOSTON

ISBN 0-8057-2424-9

MANUFACTURED IN THE UNITED STATES OF AMERICA

For

ELEANOR

*whose interest in German literature
is exceeded only by devotion to her
husband and to Christopher, Michael,
John, and Jane*

Contents

About the Author

George Wallis Field is on the faculty of the Department of German at Victoria College, University of Toronto, where he earned his M.A. and Ph.D. degrees, after graduate study also at U.C.L.A. He has edited volumes of Theodor Fontane and Heinrich Heine and is the author of a number of articles on Schiller, Thomas Mann and Hermann Hesse in such periodicals as *Monatshefte, Queen's Quarterly, The German Quarterly, University of Toronto Quarterly, German Life and Letters.* Since 1951 he has concentrated on the study of Hermann Hesse whom he visited in Montagnola in 1957, five years before Hesse's death.

Preface

Among German prose writers of the twentieth century, Hermann Hesse has been the object of a greater amount of critical literature than any save Thomas Mann and Franz Kafka. Yet the name of Hesse is not nearly as well known in the English-speaking world as those of his two compatriots. If the present study helps, in some degree, to stimulate interest in Hesse's work and to assist students of German and comparative literature, its major aim will have been achieved. A secondary aim has been to join in the continuing debate on important aspects of interpretation and critical judgment.

In a book of this length it has not been possible to present all the problems and phases of Hesse's work. I have attempted to deal with the major works as fully as possible, while at the same time trying to give a total picture of Hesse's personality and his output in many genres. Thus Chapter Nine deals briefly with the lyric poet, the literary critic, and the political thinker and essayist, Chapter Five concentrates on three major *novellas*, and in the early part of Chapter Six some attention is paid to a *Märchen* which bears on the discussion of *Siddhartha*. The first three chapters deal with the biographical background and the major and minor works of the first decade and a half in Hesse's literary career.

My debt to the legion of Hesse scholars who have preceded me is obvious and is gratefully acknowledged. Three among them deserve especial mention: Theodore Ziolkowski, Mark Boulby, and Joseph Mileck. The significance of their work extends far beyond North America, but since it is written in English, it forms the scholarly basis for the growing American interest in Hesse.

The quality of the published English translation of Hesse has been extremely deficient, although the situation has improved since the simultaneous appearance of two revised versions of *Steppenwolf* in 1963. I have used my own translations throughout and used the German titles of Hesse's works (with translations where required).

The vast secondary material has posed a problem in compiling the Selected Bibliography. Included are the major bibliographies and a number of the more useful and general items in German and French. Critical works in English are given wider representation but here, too, attention is focused on general interpretation. Specialized articles relevant to the problems discussed in the book are included.

I wish to acknowledge my gratitude to Victoria College for sabbatical leave and to the Canada Council for a travel grant which enabled me to study the *Hesse-Nachlass* in the Schiller-Nationalmuseum in 1966.

Acknowledgement is gratefully made to Suhrkamp Verlag for permission to quote from Hesse's work, and to Farrar, Straus & Giroux for permission to print the poems in Chapter Nine; to Dr. Bernhard Zeller and the Schiller-Nationalmuseum for permission to quote from *Neue deutsche Bücher* and from unpublished material in the *Hesse-Nachlass;* and Cornell University Press for permission to quote from Mark Boulby's book.

My thanks are due to Professor Sylvia Bowman, General Editor, and Professor Ulrich Weisstein, Editor of the German section of TWAS for patient and helpful answers to many queries; to my colleagues Professors Hermann Boeschenstein and C. N. Genno for reading the manuscript; and last but not least to Mrs. E. MacGregor and Miss Julie Vernie for their accurate typing of the manuscript.

GEORGE WALLIS FIELD

Victoria College, Toronto

Chronology

1877 July 2, Herman Hesse, the son of former missionaries in India, born in Calw, Württemberg.
1881– In Basel, Switzerland, where the father, Johannes, teaches
1886 at the Mission School.
1886 Return to Calw.
1891 July, passes the *Landesexamen.·*
1891 September, enters *Klosterschule* Maulbronn.
1892 March, flight from the school, followed by release in May.
1892– Pupil in the *Gymnasium*, Bad Cannstatt.
1893
1894– Apprentice in Perrot's tower clock factory in Calw.
1895
1895– Book trade apprentice in Heckenhauer's book store in
1898 Tübingen. Ludwig Finckh and le petit cénacle.
1899 *Romantische Lieder. Eine Stunde hinter Mitternacht.*
1899– Book trade in Basel. Travels in Switzerland and Italy.
1903
1901 *Hinterlassene Schriften und Gedichte von Hermann Lauscher.*
1902 *Gedichte.*
1904 *Peter Camenzind.* Marries Maria Bernoulli.
1904– Gaienhofen on the Bodensee. Free-lance writer and
1912 collaborator on a number of journals.
1906 *Unterm Rad.*
1910 *Gertrud.*
1907– Co-editor of *März.*
1912
1911 Journey to India with the painter Hans Sturzenegger.
1912– Berne, rents house of the deceased painter Albert Welti.
1919 Friendship with Romain Rolland.
1913 *Aus Indien.*
1914 *Rosshalde.*
1914– Active in relief work for prisoners and internees.

1919
1915   *Knulp*
1916   Father's death. Serious illness of wife and son Martin. Sojourn in sanatorium Sonmatt near Lucerne. Psychoanalytic sessions with Dr. J. B. Lang.
1919   *Demian. Märchen. Zarathustras Wiederkehr.*
1919– Co-editor *Vivos voco.*
1922
1919   Moves to Montagnola without family.
1920   *Blick ins Chaos.* "Klingsors letzter Sommer."
1922   *Siddhartha.*
1923   Divorce. Swiss citizenship.
1924   Second marriage, to Ruth Wenger. *Kurgast.*
1927   *Die Nürnberger Reise. Der Steppenwolf.* Second divorce.
1928   *Betrachtungen. Krisis.*
1930   *Narziss und Goldmund.* Resignation from Prussian Academy.
1931   Marriage to Ninon Dolbin, née Ausländer. Move into the Casa Rosa, built for Hesse's lifetime use by H. C. Bodmer. Beginning of *Das Glasperlenspiel.*
1932   *Die Morgenlandfahrt*
1936   *Stunden im Garten.* Gottfried-Keller Prize.
1937   *Gedenkblätter. Neue Gedichte.*
1942   *Die Gedichte.*
1943   *Das Glasperlenspiel.*
1946   Frankfurt Goethe Prize. Nobel Prize. *Dank an Goethe. Krieg und Frieden.*
1947   Honorary doctorate, Berne.
1950   Wilhelm-Raabe Prize.
1951   *Späte Prosa. Briefe.*
1955   Peace Prize of the German Book Trade. Order Pour le mérite. *Beschwörungen.*
1957   *Gesammelte Schriften* in seven vols.
1962   August 9, sudden death in Montagnola from a cerebral hemorrhage.

CHAPTER 1

Origins and Early Years

ALL of Hesse's work is autobiographical to an unusual degree even in German literature, which has been so strongly influenced by Goethe ("all my works are fragments of a great confession"), by the tradition of Romantic subjectivism, and by the pattern of the *Bildungsroman* (novel of individual development). We must, therefore, investigate Hesse's life to the extent necessary for elucidation of the works. This biographical survey becomes increasingly concerned with ideas and attitudes rather than external events.

It is tempting to divide Hesse's life into distinct periods defined by such crises as the First World War and the advent of Hitler. This is convenient and useful up to a point, provided we do not lose sight of the continued organic growth of the personality which unifies the work. Of the first prose sketches published in *Hermann Lauscher* (1899), Boulby observes:

Like Goethe's Werther, Lauscher has to die to free his author for more and, one hopes, for better things. But he leaves behind him a gene which dictates the structure of all the rest of Hesse's work—a divided self, dark and light, passionate and ironical, confessional and observing, dreaming and analytical, listening to the subterranean dreams of childhood with the ear of the critical mind. [1]

It is tempting also to portray his life as a success story—from *Heimatdichter* to *Weltbürger* (or local boy makes good)—showing his emergence as from an enfolding cocoon of narrow pietism buried in the heart of the Black Forest where he was born in the little town of Calw. In truth, Hesse had not only within himself but in his family background the widely disparate elements which probably provided the major drive for his restless creativity throughout his long life.

Pious and narrow as Hesse's home life seemed to be, his parents came from opposite ends of the German-speaking world. The father, Johannes Hesse (1847–1916), was a Baltic German, son of a locally prominent district doctor in the then Russian province of Estonia; he was technically a Russian subject and holder of the Imperial Russian title State Councillor. This doughty doctor, whose ancestors came from Thomas Mann's Hanseatic city of Lübeck, lived to be ninety-four. In fact, one can see a parallel between the religious preoccupation of the middle generation of Buddenbrooks and that which developed in Dr. Carl Hermann Hesse and reached full bloom in his son Johannes. Like "Jean" Buddenbrook this robust pioneering physician in the Baltic backwoods combined religiosity with a pragmatism as characteristic of the medical profession as it is of the Hanseatic merchant. Dr. Hesse, when well up in his eighties, climbed a tree in his garden to cut off a limb which crashed to the ground with the venerable octogenarian who, however, was unharmed. The son, Johannes, like Hanno Buddenbrook, was of less robust constitution and had a more spiritual disposition. Having resolved to place himself at God's disposal, he wrote to the Basel Mission: "My name is Johannes Hesse, I am 18 and in my final year at the *Ritter- und Domschule* in Reval. Two years ago I resolved to study theology . . . but gradually a yearning took possession of me to serve the Lord practically . . . and to follow his banner." [2]

After less than four years on the Malabar coast, weakened by malaria and dysentery, Johannes Hesse was posted to Calw as editor of the Mission magazine, and here he met and married Marie Gundert, the widow of a missionary named Isenberg with two almost grown boys.

The Gunderts were an old Swabian family with roots deep in the *Landeskirche* of Württemberg and its "monastic" schools, which were "prep" schools for the famous protestant theological faculty in Tübingen—the *Tübinger Stift*. But in 1836 Hermann Gundert (both grandfathers were named Hermann) had gone to the Malabar coast as a pioneer in this mission field. After decades in the East he became director of the Mission's publishing house in Calw and produced his dictionary of Malayalam, a prodigious pioneering effort in this area of philology. Hermann Gundert had met and married a fellow missionary in India, Julie Dubois, a French-speaking Swiss. In India, English was the common language, and, in fact, Hesse's maternal grandmother never fully mastered German and wrote in rather quaint English with French imprint to her absent husband, announcing the birth of the future poet:

I have just seen the big Hermännle who cries for hunger turning his head on every side with the mouth opened trying to get to drink. The nurse gave him a little camomille, but the portion was not sufficient for so an hungry big fellow. Adele and the boys are delighted of the brother.

We see two poles clearly reflected here: the secluded, narrow pietistic horizon of the missionary society and the isolated small town on one side and on the other the heterogeneous origins and linguistic backgrounds of Hesse's parents and grandparents. It would also be an oversimplification to call the missionary outlook and experience narrow. Travel broadens, and this applies to most missionary careers. Hesse's boyhood home, so far from the beaten track, was something like the crossroads of the world, for there was a stream of visitors from abroad including Englishmen and Indians. The boy resented English when spoken by his parents in order to conceal something from the children. At the time, French generally had preference over English in the schools of southern Germany, and so Hesse's linguistic skills were developed mainly in Latin (he later translated and published the medieval Latin of Cäsarius von Heisterbach), Greek, French, and only a little English. Hesse wrote me before his death:

I often read French in younger years. English I never understood well enough to read good literature in the original. My parents and sisters spoke English fluently, there were also many English and American visitors in our house. But my English reading consisted only of some light literature for practice, a little Mark Twain, a little Kipling.

In translation I read a great deal of English literature and among recent authors esteemed Hardy, Meredith, Virginia Woolf, Forster and many others.

Hermann was the second child of six, of whom only four survived to maturity: his older sister Adele, a younger sister Marulla, and a brother Hans, whose suicide in the nineteen-thirties came as a shock, for it took place when the two brothers were enjoying a rare reunion.

Remarks in parental letters and diaries and Hesse's own writings reveal a gifted but "difficult," headstrong child who in the° local Latin School found "only a single teacher whom I loved and to whom I can be grateful." [3]

Between Hesse's third and ninth years the family had lived in Basel and acquired Swiss citizenship; and when at fourteen he was to sit for the *Landesexamen,* which opened for the top two dozen boys the way to a free education in the theological preparatory schools and the *Tübinger Stift,* he had to be naturalized as a subject of the King of Württemberg. Even before winning his place in the former fourteenth-century Cistercian monastery at Maulbronn, Hesse had, at thirteen, resolved "to be a poet or nothing." [4]

Behind this boyish resolution lay the divergent worlds of his forebears and the disparate aspects of his environment: a situation conducive to pulsation between poles of insularity and cosmopolitan awareness. But even in the narrow confines of his family he found inspiration for this decision in his mother's storytelling, and he later paid tribute to her "moving art" and the "inexhaustible wellspring of her lips."

Of his father Hesse recalled that as a Baltic Russo-German he never assimilated Swabian and Swiss dialects but went right on speaking "his pure, cultivated, beautiful High German. We loved this High German very much and were proud of it . . . just as we loved and were proud of the slim, frail, delicate figure, the noble high brow and the pure, often suffering look in his eyes, which were nevertheless always true and open and summoning to good behavior and chivalrous conduct, appealing to our better nature." [5]

In his father, Hesse found the model for a pure prose style, but from his mother he acquired the warmth and vigor of the Swabian dialect, a vivid imagination and great musicality, for she had a beautiful voice and was devoted to music, while the father could not sing at all. Throughout his life, Hesse wrote and spoke with only a slight trace of Swabian—enough to give individual strength and color to his idiom.

The boy's early reading must also have led him towards his poetic ambition. He had two large libraries at his disposal: his father's and also that of Grandfather Gundert. All the classic and standard authors were represented, and, of course, both his father and his grandfather were constantly employed in writing, editing, and publishing.

At fourteen, with a place in the Maulbronn Preparatory Seminary, Hesse's future seemed fixed in the orbit of Lutheran pastors and missionaries. Hölderlin, Hegel, and Mörike had gone through the system, but their names are remembered to the extent that they broke with it or transcended it. The usual career meant an education at the state's expense followed, inexorably, by ordination in the Lutheran State Church and a pastoral charge or teaching position. At first, the young seminarist found it fun to translate Ovid into German hexameters. In German composition he was first in his class. His letters reported that Homer was magnificent and that he was on the best of terms with pupils and teachers (except for the teacher of music and gymnastics).

In the middle of March 1892—six months, after having entered the school—this apparently model pupil ran away and was brought back, half-frozen, by a rural constable. In the following months, his depression became alarming, and in May his father removed him from the school. He was put in the care of a theologian who seems to have combined the functions of exorcist and psychiatrist. From an institution near Stuttgart he was transferred to one in Basel and finally the boy was allowed to attend the *Gymnasium* in Bad Cannstatt; but after a year this attempt to give him an academic education failed. After several months at home helping his father, his parents reluctantly consented to his apprenticeship in the local tower-clock factory. After a year and a half—during which his reading developed further—he was apprenticed to a bookstore in Tübingen. These events are reflected in Hesse's second novel *Unterm Rad*.

Hesse was at home in the world of books, and his new master was a wise and indulgent employer who allowed ample freedom to his apprentice. By this time, some of Hesse's former schoolmates had arrived in Tübingen as students. Sometimes he felt like an outsider among his friends who had matriculated into the university. At other times, he took a loftier view and considered himself above the business of academic learning and student behavior. In his last two years in Tübingen, he belonged to a literary circle called "le petit cénacle," which included his closest friend Ludwig Finckh, who was later known as "der Rosendoktor" after the title of his only really successful novel.

In his four years in Tübingen, Hesse rigorously pursued his self-education. Goethe became the center of his interests, and he later wrote in *Dank an Goethe* (1932): "Among all German poets, Goethe is the one to whom I owe most, the one who has preoccupied me most, oppressed me and encouraged me, forced me to follow his path or rebel against it." Then he turned to the Romantics, to Brentano, Eichendorff, Tieck, Schleiermacher, Schlegel, and especially Jean Paul and Novalis. Not only their works and their letters but histories of literature and critical works as well were systematically studied by this avid self-taught student.

In this brief summary of the first two decades of his life we have met clues that will return again and again in Hesse's confessional writings. The milieu and external events which recur in various disguises are less important than the themes and psychological motifs which emerge from these years of crisis. The dominant theme is that of individual development and self-fulfillment summed up in the motto of *Demian:*

After all, I wanted only to attempt to live that which was trying to work its way out of me. Why was that so terribly difficult?

This urge to express and develop what is within the individual leads directly to a second, associated theme, namely, constant change or transcendence. From Peter Camenzind to Joseph Knecht in *Das Glasperlenspiel* we see characters casting off their old self and entering new stages of awareness and being.[6] This suggests at once an affinity with certain aspects of existentialist thought. This restless effort to express what is within and the constant evolution which accompanies it are deeply rooted in the author and the struggles of his early years.

All three elements—the confessional basis, the self-development, the constant striving for newer and higher stages of being—although inherent in Hesse's psyche and personal experience, relate him at once to Goethe and place him in a traditional stream. There is peculiar irony in the situation in which the iconoclast and revolutionary finds himself the inheritor of a long tradition even in these respects. It is not surprising, therefore, that we find an oscillation in Hesse's work between conservative, traditional and dissenting, revolutionary patterns and attitudes. This can be seen as another major motif running through most of his work.

CHAPTER 2

Romanticism and Rebellion

I Romantische Lieder

H ESSE'S first published work was a poem, "Madonna," printed
in a Viennese journal in 1896; and his first book, published
in 1898 at his own expense (now a rare collector's item), was a
volume of poems, *Romantische Lieder*. He continued to write
poems to the last day of his life, and although he attempted
different styles—e.g. the uncompromising starkness, self-lacera-
tion and dissonance of *Krisis* (1927)—on the whole the poetic
side of his work shows, throughout his life, the Romantic and
folksong tradition. From an early age, he was attracted to music
and wrote to his parents from Tübingen that he regretted
having insufficient time to practice the violin. A clue to the
nature of his work whether in prose or verse is found in the
kind of music which interested Hesse at different periods.
Romantische Lieder, for instance, stands under the aegis of
Chopin. In 1897 he wrote to his parents:

What Wagner meant to Nietzsche, Chopin means to me, or even
more. With these warm, living melodies, with this piquant sensuous,
nervous harmony, with all this exceptionally intimate music of Chopin
everything basic in my intellectual and spiritual life is connected. And

then I am continually amazed by the dignity of Chopin, the restraint, the perfected control of his nature. In him everything is noble, even though much is decadent.[1]

An air of *fin-de-siècle* decadence and estheticism pervades these early works. "I have been absolutely convinced for some time," the same letter continues, "that morality is replaced by esthetics in the artist." The title of the first poem, "An die Schönheit," strikes this note; and its third stanza evokes echoes of Romantic isolation, longing for the infinite and the ideal, of melancholy and withdrawal from "green and gold" into the dark river of time and night:

> Tänze und Gefahren sanken
> In den dunklen Fluss der Zeit,
> Ohne Nähen, ohne Schranken
> Wölbt sich meine Einsamkeit.
> Grün und Gold und Himmel schwand;
> Ueberm Ufer meiner kranken
> Seele liegt mein Heimwehland.[2]

Even before the volume appeared, the poet replied to his mother's rather critical appraisal of the manuscript, stating that he was past this stage: "I have since become more independent, calmer and clearer."

We shall later attempt an evaluation of Hesse's place as a lyric poet. For the present, it suffices to note that the mood and style of these early poems is carried over into his first prose works. The volume of poetry of which hardly any copies were sold did attract the attention of the Leipzig publisher Diedrichs who invited Hesse to submit to him his next manuscript.

In 1899 nine prose sketches appeared under the title *Eine Stunde hinter Mitternacht*. The title was taken from a verse of one of the *Romantische Lieder*. This stylized early prose, with its aura of estheticism and decadence and its cultivation of Romantic clichés, holds little attraction for the general reader today. But for the Hesse scholar there is some fascination in tracing here the origins of basic themes and images that were to run through the author's later work. The ambivalent relationship of the real and the ideal is prefigured, for example, in the first sketch, "Island Dream": "What you see here is more beautiful than all reality, and more real than all reality," and the opening paragraph contains the Narcissus symbol: "My reflected image lay spread out in the dark green still waters of the inlet."

In this year, having served his apprenticeship with Heckenhauer in Tübingen, Hesse took a position in a bookstore in Basel. He reveled in the atmosphere of this ancient city made famous by Arnold Böcklin, Burckhardt and Nietzsche, whose works Hesse carried in his luggage. He had read Schopenhauer, too, but at this time he was still too much under the spell of Nietzsche to be fully responsive to Jacob Burckhardt, who as Pater Jacobus was later to play such an important role in *Das Glasperlenspiel.*

In the second volume of prose sketches, *Hermann Lauscher* (1901), we find no longer a constant Romantic melancholy but an alternation between fantasy and reality. This oscillation is a feature of those late and rather independent Romantics, E.T.A. Hoffmann and Jean Paul, but it is also an indication of Hesse's emergence from the imitative, Romantic pattern towards finding himself. This interplay between the real and the unreal was later to form the basic structure of *Steppenwolf.*

II Peter Camenzind

In 1903 *Hermann Lauscher* brought an invitation from S. Fischer to submit any new work; and it was under this famous publisher's imprint that *Peter Camenzind* appeared in 1904. This first novel was an instant success. While there is a good deal of Romantic reveling in nature and sentimentality, *Peter Camenzind* marks a breakthrough to a more robust and humorous style. Some of the humor may lack subtlety but that, too, is in keeping with the youthful freshness pervading this novel. Perhaps the funniest scene is that of the prohibitionists parading through the city led by a standard-bearer who, wearied by the long dry speeches on the evils of drink, had consoled himself in the nearest pub and is now reduced to a staggering gait as he reels drunkenly through the streets, proudly waving the blue-cross banner of total abstinence. Another episode suggestive of Hesse's later irony is the humorous juxtaposition of Wagner's *Tristan* and Swiss yodeling.

In a letter addressed in 1951 to a student working on *Peter Camenzind,* Hesse pointed to the basic theme: "Camenzind is striving away from the world and society back to nature; he is repeating on a small scale the half valiant, half sentimental revolt of Rousseau. In this way he becomes a poet." [3] The fact that Camenzind becomes a poet is not so much apparent in the novel's ending as in the novelist's development, thus pointing to the autobiographical element. Hesse went on to point out the "beginning of the red thread through all my work":

His [Camenzind's] aim and ideal is not to become a brother in a band, colleague in a conspiracy, voice in a choir. On the contrary, in place of community, comradeship, and integration, he seeks the opposite. He is intent on walking not the path of the many but, obstinately, on his own individual course. He does not want to run with the many and adapt. . . .

The sincerity of the hero's search for his own way gives the book its impact even today. On the other hand, the social criticism rests on shaky foundations. The tragic end of the friend Richard by drowning smacks of sentimentality, and the ineffectual efforts of Peter to bridge the gulf between himself and the opposite sex must seem far-fetched to today's uninhibited youth. The spirit of St. Francis of Assisi—protector of all living things—was a major influence in Hesse's life at this time (after his first Italian journey), but here it is oddly at variance with a certain Nietzschean drive to separate from the heard. Peter's devoted care of the cripple Boppi represents this Franciscan subordination of the individual to the service of mankind, whereas Peter ends in an isolated hermit's existence in the high mountains to live and carve out his own life uninfluenced and undisturbed by others.

But where they are part of the author's experience, these elements, undigested and ill-assorted as they may be, are so powerfully expressed that the reader is almost convinced. Only the criticism of life in Paris, which Hesse never visited, comes off badly:

Paris was frightful: Nothing but art, politics, literature and harlots' lingerie, nothing but artists, literati, politicians, and low women. The artists were as vain and importunate as the politicians, the literati even more vain and importunate and the women most vain and importunate of all. [4]

Peter lives in Basel in the kind of quarters which Hesse occupied. The illness and death of Peter's mother Marie reflect the death of Hesse's mother in 1902. Like Hesse, Peter hikes through Northern Italy and absorbs the spirit of St. Francis and the humble peasants. These locales are vividly re-evoked:

> I walked the ways of Saint Francis and, at times, felt him walking beside me, his soul full of unfathomable love, greeting every bird and every spring and every dog-rose with joy and gratitude. I plucked and consumed lemons on glistening sundrenched slopes, sojourned in little villages, sang and composed inwardly and celebrated Easter in Assisi, in the church of my saint. (I, 290)

It may strike us as odd, however, that two paragraphs later the anti-cultural, anti-social tendency of the book comes to the fore amid the glories of Italian art and architecture:

> But in Florence I felt for the first time the whole shabby ridiculousness of modern culture. There for the first time I was overcome by the presentiment that I would also be a stranger in our society, and there the wish first awakened in me to lead my life outside this society and if possible in the south.

This first novel thus brings out strongly the "outsider" theme, which in subsequent works was to be developed under many aspects. The theme accounts in part for the following Hesse's works have found among disaffected and disenchanted young people. But the lasting, wider appeal of this first novel lies in the relentless pursuit of the search for his own identity. Social integration in Basel, Italy, or Paris, friendship, love, the possibility of marriage, music, art, academic pursuits, even writing—all these Peter attempts and rejects:

> I often looked in astonishment at these people who greeted me as an unusual guest and of whom I knew that they saw one another precisely so many times a week. What did they talk about and what did they do in each other's company? Most of them represented the same stereotype form of *homo socialis,* and they seemed to me all somewhat alike, by virtue of a social and leveling mentality, which I alone did not possess. (I, 302)

Passages such as this anticipate the "outsider" theme in contemporary literature portraying existentialist *Angst* and isolation in the midst of mass urban society. But the sincerity, seriousness, and Nietzschean relentlessness of the search for the self is balanced by the humorous note which is explicitly part of Camenzind's quest—thus anticipating *Steppenwolf*: "Now I gradually acquired an eye for the humor of life" (I, 324).

With ironic humor, Peter describes a hypersensitive esthete who fell into the hands of a rascal of a Maecenas:

> In the wealthy man's villas he carried on a stale esthetic bragging with the ladies, rose in his own imagination to the status of an unrecognized hero and, woefully misled through sheer Chopin music and Pre-Raphaelite ecstasies, systematically lost his reason. (I, 283)

Beneath the stridencies of Camenzind's observations we are aware that Hesse has passed beyond the short-lived esthetic phase of the *Romantische Lieder* and his predilection for Chopin. With its emphasis on the quest of the individual for maturity and self-knowledge, *Peter Camenzind* belongs in the tradition of the *Bildungsroman*, but in an almost inverse sense, since the goal of his training and experience could be described as anti-*Bildung*, ending in a misanthropic Rousseauistic return to nature.

III Unterm Rad

A large part of Hesse's next novel was written during a lengthy visit to Calw in 1903–1904. Meanwhile, the success of *Peter Camenzind* enabled Hesse to retire from the bookstore and to marry Maria Bernoulli, who had been in the group with which Hesse had made another trip to Florence in 1903. Nine years older than he, she was only distantly related to the prominent Basel family of mathematicians and scholars. She was an accomplished pianist, and especially devoted to Chopin. In several shorter prose pieces and poems Hesse described her playing of Chopin. But the disharmony that, before long, was to appear in this marriage is reflected in Hesse's changing musical taste; and we have seen that as early as *Camenzind* he was emerging from his enchantment with this music.

With the novel *Unterm Rad* (*Beneath the Wheel*) Hesse returned to his Calw and Göppingen school days and the Maulbronn fiasco. The full extent of this early crisis in Hesse's life has recently been revealed by the publication of relevant documents.[5] While boarding in *Präzeptor* Geiger's house and attending the *Gymnasium* in the Stuttgart suburb of Cannstatt, the fifteen-year-old Hesse wrote to his mother on January 20, 1893:

> Every letter you send shows that you understand me or at least my letters quite incorrectly . . .
> N.B. If I had all the "Holy Ghost" you wish me, I would long since have become a great apostle.
> And your "God" too! To be sure it may be that he exists, and he may even be just the way you picture him to yourself, but he doesn't interest me. It's no use thinking you can influence me in that way.
>
> • • •
>
> I am interested in nothing. Day after day I am talked at, about languages, constitutions, wars, nations, statistics, hypotheses, experiments, emperors, forces, electroscopes, and whatever the garbage is called—and I listen; some things I retain, others I don't, and the whole business couldn't mean less to me. . . . I could become a Ph.D., a professor, perhaps even a kind of *Studienrat* who is privileged to be dumb and to carry around a big belly and wear a silk waistcoat with a golden watch-chain. . . .
>
> • • •
>
> This afternoon I had another nasty attack like the one in Basel. I was sitting here reading Eichendorff; suddenly the whole ugly old [illegible] came over me, the gloomy melancholy, the griping love pang. . . . I grabbed some books at random and sold them in Stuttgart for—a revolver. And now I am sitting here again and the rusty weapon is lying in front of me.
> I have gained control of myself this time, or else I was a coward! I don't know; but my head is full of noise and confusion, and I wish I knew someone to whom I could say: Help me!

For any mother the shock of receiving such a letter from a fifteen-year-old son would be great. For Marie Hesse, with her absolute faith and devout missionary background, the shock and pain were profound. She recorded in her diary:

> On January 21 I traveled to Cannstatt, since Hermann had written that he had sold some schoolbooks and bought a pistol, as life was too great a burden. Find him very sick, angry, unhappy. Geiger noticed nothing. Sleep in the small room next to him. The

Sunday morning was terrible . . . the terrible excitement of Hermann who screamed abuse at me so that I would have preferred to leave at once. Then when he had become friendly and approachable at the station and I wanted a little more time alone with him, we were disturbed by the Masers . . . father . . . prays a great deal for Hermann, but he cannot and will not advise. Only God can help here.[6]

The correspondence of the following weeks and months reflects ups and downs with constant reference to recurring headaches. Shortly after the beginning of the following autumn term, the situation became critical, and Hesse wrote to his parents in October, 1893: "I don't think I can go on any longer. All day I have not exactly full-blown headaches but a constant dull and terrible pressure in my head that becomes a real headache if I try any concentrated work."

The boy was taken home and on October 27 entered a bookstore in Esslingen as apprentice. After three days he ran away and was picked up in Stuttgart by his father. After many consultations, he was allowed to help in the garden and in his father's editorial work until June, when he expressed a willingness to become an apprentice in Perrot's clock factory in Calw.

These personal experiences are strikingly reflected in the novel *Unterm Rad;* but even more striking are the circumstances that indicate the author's *Distanzierung.* Hesse waited for more than a decade for these episodes in his life to simmer down before he effected an esthetic distillation. The most striking differences in the hero's situation are the complete absence of a mother figure in Hans Giebenrath's world (although the mothers of other boys are described delivering their sons to Maulbronn), the complete alteration of the image of the father, and the absence of religious or theological background in the immediate family. Moreover Hesse himself has indicated that Hans Giebenrath is a reflection of his younger brother Hans: "The preparatory school, which had also caused me a lot of conflicts, became a tragedy for him as time went on. . . . In the story [*Unterm Rad*] the painful school career of my brother was almost as important a source as my own" (IV, 702).

In this work Hesse for the first time used two figures to reflect two different aspects of himself. Hans Giebenrath reflects Hesse's boyhood in the Latin school in Calw, his success in the *Landesexamen,* and the first months at the Preparatory School at Maulbronn. But it was Hermann Heilner who rebelled against the system and ran away like Hesse—presumably, as Heilner (Heiler=healer) suggests, in order to go on to better things and eventual success as a poet and novelist. Hans's subsequent decline and removal from Maulbronn and his apprenticeship reflect Hesse's experiences perhaps in a more acute form. The death of Hans—whether by accidental drowning or by suicide is immaterial—is in line with the theme: that the educational system is bad and blights the potential in a gifted youth. The reader of the novel must remember that the absent friend Heilner is probably fending for himself and carving out a place for himself through his pen.

Unterm Rad owed part of its immediate success to the fact that it rode a wave of school novels criticizing the educational system and the establishment and dealing with the crises of puberty and adolescence: Emil Strauss's *Freund Hein* (1902), Robert Musil's *Die Verwirrungen des Zöglings Törless* (1906), and Heinrich Mann's *Professor Unrat* (1905), and similar works. Indeed, some of Thomas Mann's stories are on the periphery of this genre: *Das Wunderkind* and *Tonio Kröger* spring to mind. But in these and, to a slightly lesser degree, in *Freund Hein* the artist theme dominates, and Hesse's novel is not primarily a *Künstlerroman*, although it is related both through the destroyed creative potential one may assume in Hans and the actual poetic gifts evident in Heilner.

Both directly and indirectly Hesse delivered a vigorous attack on the educational system: indirectly, because the reader is filled with compassion for Hans in the crushing fate which relentlessly destroys him. But in many passages the attack becomes a direct broadside:

A schoolmaster would rather have ten notorious asses in his class than one genius—and thus from school to school the scene of battle between law and spirit (*Geist*) is repeated, and over and over again we see the state and the school breathlessly intent on crushing at the root the few deeper and more deserving minds that crop up from year to year.

In more recent editions the reader will look in vain for these lines. The passage was purged to read, following the dash:

—and when one looks at the situation closely he [the schoolmaster] is right, for it is not his task to develop extravagant minds but rather to produce good Latin scholars, mathematicians, and sturdy citizens [*Biedermänner*].'

The revision is so drastic that it practically condones the situation which originally was under such heavy attack. Hesse's youthful rebellion mellowed with age and finally left him in *Das Glasperlenspiel* in more explicit sympathy with the teacher. But even in the first version of *Unterm Rad* there is a note of ambivalence in the educational picture. In an early stage of his education,

Hans began to glimpse the riddles and tasks that lay hidden in every verse and word, he began to perceive how through the ages thousands of scholars, thinkers, and researchers had struggled with these questions, and it seemed to him that he himself was being received into this circle of seekers after truth. (I, 416)

Such passages presage the reception of the acolyte in the Castalian order. In the latter portion of *Unterm Rad,* there is no longer any occasion for praise of the scholar and teacher. The illiterate lay preacher, shoemaker Flaig, is the foil by which the shifting emphasis may be measured. At first Hans looks down upon him from his scholarly position, but in the end Flaig's hostility to learning and to the establishment—especially the theological establishment—seems justified. Near the end, Hans lingers outside the shoemaker's house observing the cosy, confined innocence of the family within:

He couldn't find the courage to enter. What would he do and say inside? He could not help thinking how as a youngster of eleven or twelve he had often come here; then Flaig had told him Biblical stories and had met his stormy, curious questions about hell, the devil, and spirits. These memories made him uncomfortable and gave him a bad conscience. He did not know what he wanted . . . but it seemed to him that he was standing before something secret and forbidden. (I, 516)

The passage makes clear the deeper philosophical implications of the situation, for Hans has left the first golden age of innocence and, badly piloted, has run aground in the turbulent seas of the middle period. The connection is made with the world of sex—something secret and forbidden—because it is through Flaig's visiting niece that Hans gains access to this mysterious realm, which also holds only rebuffs and disillusionment for him. Here, too, Hans in his depressed state seems to meet failure and rejection, and this episode marks another step towards the tragic end.

Unterm Rad remains a moving work in which atmosphere, symbols, and allusions gather monumentum to foreshadow the tragic end. It sensitively probes the psychological problems of the adolescent. In doing so, Hesse has painted a realistic picture of a way of life in the small town of Calw at the turn of the century. The novel is his *Werther*, expelling from his innermost being this traumatic sequence. As a critique of society and, particularly of the educational system, it is ambivalent, even before the later excisions were made. For the protagonist, it is hinted, bears within him traits of physical and psychological weakness so that the blame for his fate may rest upon himself: "A trained modern observer remembering the mother's fragile nature and the long family history might have mentioned hypertrophy of intelligence as a symptom of incipient degeneration" (I, 376).

The novel marks an advance beyond *Peter Camenzind*, not only in its greater realism but also in its basic retraction of *Camenzind's* Rousseauistic return to natural man. For implicit in Hans's story and its imagery is the awareness that it is impossible to go back and begin again. To do so is pathological regression, neurosis: "When a tree is cut, it often produces new shoots near the roots . . . but it is a deceptive vitality for they will never grow into a proper tree" (I, 495). Boulby has analyzed this situation perceptively:

> *Beneath the Wheel* on its deepest level is unconsciously the most pessimistic novel Hesse ever wrote, for it alone denies completely the value of the inward way. . . . Apparently an aggressive, "Romantic" satire, it is actually a further step outward beyond *Peter Camenzind* toward "realism," toward bourgeois compromise.[8]

I find it difficult, however, to accept Boulby's adverse judgment on its literary quality: "As a work of art the novel might even be adjudged a serious disappointment after *Peter Camenzind*, having all the distinguishing marks of a minor talent." [9] For despite its faults, its exaggerations and polemics, the work seems to me an advance upon its predecessor with as many distinguishing marks of genius as of minor talent. As a reviewer of the French translation declared in 1958: "Il s'agit d'une oeuvre de jeunesse . . . Mais [elle] a ses beautés et témoigne d'une maîtrise tôt acquise." [10]

CHAPTER 3

The Artist Novels: Gertrud *and* Rosshalde

I *By Lake Constance*

AS with Thomas Mann, the artist theme is never far from Hesse's works, and we have seen how this personal problem formed part of the thematic texture of *Peter Camenzind* and *Unterm Rad*. But in the decade with which the present chapter deals, Hesse was more acutely aware of the problem in his own life.

Hesse and his bride, looking for an idyllic country spot, finally decided upon Gaienhofen on the German shore of Lake Constance, where they rented an unused peasant cottage, in which their first son, Bruno, was born in 1905. The primitive living conditions were now felt more acutely, and so they resolved to build in an isolated location outside the village, not far from Ludwig Finckh, who had now published his novel *Der Rosendoktor*. In the new location, the garden became for Hesse at first a relaxing recreation and then gradually a time-consuming burden. Only many years later did he return to this pastime with delight (Cf. *Stunden im Garten*, 1936).

The withdrawn mode of life may not have been propitious for this marriage, which was destined to break up after a dozen years. In any event, Hesse soon felt domesticity to be incompatible with his calling as an artist, and this is manifest already in the first *Künstlerroman, Gertrud,* in 1910.

In his rural retreat Hesse was not entirely isolated, however. Musicians and painters were frequent guests, and trips were made to the opera and to concerts in Konstanz across the lake. Among the writers who came to Hesse's house were Stefan Zweig, Bruno Frank, Wilhelm Schäfer, and Emil Strauss.

The number of written and published works in this apparently idyllic period is staggering. During the Gaienhofen years (1905–12) appeared *Diesseits* (five tales, 1907), *Nachbarn* (five tales, 1908), *Aus Indien* (notes and poems written on Hesse's trip to the East, 1913), and the novel *Gertrud* (1910). But the mention of these books by no means completes the picture of Hesse's literary activity. He had published his first book review in Basel and after his rise to prominence in 1904 was increasingly sought as a reviewer. He was a constant contributor to such journals as *Die Rheinlande, Propyläen, Simplicissimus,* and during these years he edited the journal *März* along with Albert Langen and Ludwig Thoma. In addition to his own books, poems, stories, essays, and reviews in these and other periodicals, Hesse edited seven books within seven years, including works of Jean Paul and Eichendorff. It is little wonder, then, that he found gardening a burden upon his time and energy. Little wonder, too, that the quality of the shorter prose fiction of this period is uneven. We shall pass over these items in order to concentrate on the best short stories in Chapter Five. Finally we may note that all three sons were born in the retreat on Lake Constance.

II Gertrud

As we have seen in the earlier novels, the preoccupation with the artist problem is an inevitable concomitant of the confessional nature of Hesse's major works. But in *Gertrud* Hesse brought this theme into the foreground and produced his most pronounced, if not his best, *Künstlerroman.* It, too, rode the crest of a wave which bore Thomas Mann's *Buddenbrooks, Tonio Kröger, Tristan, Death in Venice,* Heinrich Mann's *Die Jagd nach Liebe,* Rilke's *Aufzeichnungen des Malte Laurids Brigge,* Hauptmann's *Michael Kramer,* and Joyce's *Portrait of the Artist as a Young Man.*

All three protagonists in *Gertrud* are in some degree artists, so that the novel presents both a clash between art and life and a conflict between different artistic temperaments and concepts. The divorce between art and life is emphasized by the choice of music, which implies a sharper dissociation from ordinary life. According to Schopenhauer, music is the most ethereal and absolute of the arts and confers a release from the ordinary process of the will. On the novel's second page, music is hailed as "a deep consolation and a justification of all life: O music! . . . for the moments that it lives in you it extinguishes in you everything that is accidental, evil, brutal, sad; it causes the world to resound with you, makes what is heavy light and lends wings to what is fixed and rigid."

Unfortunately, the posthumous publication of the fragment *Gertrud*[1] throws little light on our finished novel, for the fragment's protagonists are an architect and a painter whose problems and situations bear little relation to those depicted in the completed work. It seems likely that Hesse abandoned the first project while retaining the title.

Near the beginning of *Gertrud*—the story is told in the first person—the narrator mentions his pleasure in improvising [phantasieren] on the violin, but "I noticed that it is one thing to delve into one's dreams and taste enchanted hours and quite another thing to wrestle clearly and relentlessly with the secrets of form as if struggling with demons. And I perceived even at that time something of the way in which real creativity isolates us and demands of us something that we have to sever from the comfort of life" (II, 14).

Kuhn, a young student of music, undistinguished from the normal healthy run-of-the-mill, is injured and crippled for life on a toboggan party. Only after he is cut off from life does his talent emerge, and in words reminiscent of Tonio Kröger watching the Danish dance of life, Kuhn reflects: "I would always stand apart as an outsider, just as at the dance, and would have to look on and be regarded by the girls as deficient, and if one of them were ever nice to me, it would be out of pity!" (II, 30).

Kuhn then turns from life to art and becomes a composer: the marked—in this case crippled—man becomes a creative artist. Opposite him stands Muoth,[2] the opera singer, the performing "artist." The two incongruous friends are rivals for Gertrud who is also highly musical, plays the piano, and sings

Kuhn's compositions. One of the faults of the book is the shadowy depiction of the title figure. The novel would have been more aptly entitled "Kuhn and Muoth," for we penetrate to the depths of their natures while we never feel that we know Gertrud's soul at all. In a letter to Conrad Haussmann, Hesse admitted "that Gertrud . . . was for me less a character than a symbol."

While Kuhn rises progressively on the ladder of creative art, Gertrud decides in favor of the extrovert, charming, sociable singer. The marriage is increasingly undermined as Muoth's gay façade is eaten away by his effort to defy time and be constantly on the pinnacle of vocal form. His alcoholism is only symptomatic of the inner struggle to keep up appearances. Like Muoth Senator Thomas Buddenbrook is also worn down by the constant effort of "representation." Muoth's problem can be expressed in esthetic and metaphysical terms. He almost anticipates existentialism as he fights against an inner awareness that he and his art face oblivion whereas the creative artist can erect a monument to defy the erosion of time. Kuhn, on the other hand, retreats still further from life after losing Gertrud to Muoth and lives more and more for his art achieving ever greater success.

Though the development of the artist theme and the psychological study of the two male artists in this novel is interesting, the book has withstood the passage of time less successfully than Hesse's other longer works of fiction. Apart from the unsatisfactory portrayal of the woman or even the woman artist, the mood of the work is insipid and sentimental: "One can only accept what falls to one's lot . . ." (II, 139). The ending is perhaps one of the least satisfying aspects. After Muoth's death, the widow Gertrud and the composer Kuhn live separate lonely lives near enough to visit and console each other. This distant contact with his beloved inspires Kuhn to further creativity. Thus separation of art and life dominates at the end: the artist needs the inspiration that can be drawn from contact with life and a loving heart, but full involvement in life, for instance by marriage, would end his creativity.

As Bernhard Zeller states, the novel—"a sentimental poetic fiction of renunciation and isolation"—met with a mixed reception. But the light it sheds on the author is of considerable interest. It reflects the end of the domination of Chopin (perhaps influenced by Hesse's friendship with the young Swiss composer Othmar Schoeck) and reveals that even in these early years of his marriage Hesse felt the incompatibility of his vocation as artist with the claims of "real" life focused on wife and children. Thus the career of the composer can be seen as another variation on the basic theme: know thyself, be thyself.

III Rosshalde

Heiner, Hesse's second son, was born in 1909, and Martin, the youngest, in 1911. By this time, Hesse felt the ties of family and home unbearably restricting and succumbed to the urging of his friend, the painter Hans Sturzenegger, to accompany him on a trip to the East Indies. The voyage was not only a flight from an uncomfortable domestic situation, for the lure of India beckoned from the past of his parents and grandparents and from his increasing preoccupation with Eastern philosophy and mythology. The peripheral figure of the theosophist Lohe in *Gertrud* gives evidence of this tendency, and Schopenhauer naturally led Hesse to India.

The travel book *Aus Indien* shows the author's disillusionment with the sordid, teeming throngs of Eastern races in Ceylon, Penang, Singapore, and Sumatra. Visiting the Buddhist temple in Kandy, Ceylon, Hesse tried in vain to let the mystic vision overcome the discomfort of dysentery. Like his father, he seemed unequal to the strain imposed by the climate and the endemic diseases and canceled his plan for a longer stay and a visit to the Malabar coast, the scene of his family's missionary endeavors. He retained a vivid impression of the "absolute strength and future" of the Chinese; but on the return journey he recorded that "most of my impressions were of a purely human nature . . . important and dear to me through their relatedness with myself and with every human being." [3]

It took Hesse ten years to forget the raw reality of life in India and to recapture the poetic, mythical, and philosophical vision of the East in *Siddhartha*. Actually, China had begun to supersede India, as is evident from the Chinese background of "Der Dichter" ("The Poet"), one of his best *Märchen* (fairy tales), first published in *Die Rheinlande* (1907).

After his return from the East, it was clear to Hesse that the life in Gaienhofen had to end: "It was pleasant and instructive, and yet became, in the end, a kind of slavery. Pretending to be peasants was fine so long as it was play: when it had grown to be a habit and a duty, it lost its appeal." [4] In expressing himself in these terms, Hesse was consciously suppressing the most difficult problem: the danger that confronted his marriage.

At the end of 1912, the Hesses rented the house of the recently deceased painter, Albert Welti, on the outskirts of Berne, and this became the *Herrensitz* (manor house) Rosshalde in another, novel entitled *Rosshalde*, portraying the dichotomy of art and life—this time in the person of the painter Veraguth. Camenzind and Heilner had been budding poets, Kuhn a composer, and now Hesse was influenced not only by the late owner of the estate and its studio but seemed to anticipate his own breakthrough into painting five years later. Interesting as the treatment of the artist theme in this work may be, it recedes before the domestic tragedy which unfolds almost with the inexorable fatality of a Greek tragedy. Autobiographical allusions are unmistakable and shattering when fully comprehended. Veraguth's older wife "was a little taller than himself, a strong figure, healthy but without youth, and although she had ceased to love her husband, even today she regarded the loss of his affection as a sad incomprehensible misfortune that had befallen her through no fault of her own" (II, 484). The wife is also a musician, and in this case there seems to be no bridge between the worlds of music and painting. She lives in the manor house while Veraguth has set up bachelor quarters in the coach house which contains his studio. A grown son, Albert, is at the university but comes home on holiday early in the story. He belongs entirely to his mother, shares her interest in music and uses this to exclude his father from a conversation about Wagner. In the first chapter, Veraguth has received a letter from his friend Burkhardt, inviting him to come to India with him. However, almost at once the story begins to focus on little Pierre, the younger son, who is the last link between the parents. Hesse heightens the impact of this tale by his sympathetic penetration into child psychology. After a conversation with his father's manservant,

> Pierre did not answer. It was always the same. If you let yourself be persuaded to talk with a grownup about something that was really important, it always ended with a disappointment or even with a humiliation. (II, 488)

The reader is so enthralled with seven-year-old Pierre and his naive, intuitive, and slightly precocious "child's eye" view that he undergoes a shattering experience in the tragedy that ensues when Pierre develops cerebral meningitis[5] and dies in agony to the anguish not only of both parents but of the reader as well. This is the end. The East beckons to a crushed Veraguth and there is no longer any point in postponing the divorce:

> What remained for him was his art, of which he had never felt so sure as now. There remained for him the solace of the outsiders who are not destined to grasp life and drink it to the full; there remained the strange, cool, yet uncontrollable passion of seeing, observing, and creating in proud isolation. That was all that was left and the only value in this shipwrecked life, this unswerving isolation and cold joy of artistic creation, and it was now his fate to follow this guiding star without detours. (II, 633)

This work marks a new advance in Hesse's development as a writer. When the author reread it for the first time after twenty-six years, he found it had passed the test of time and that in it he had perfected his technique. He went on to observe that it was just as well that the war tore him away from this development to lead him into problems before which the purely esthetic factors dwindled in significance.

In *Rosshalde* there are no vestiges of Romantic vagueness and sentimentality. The style is crisp, clear, and concise—even clinical in detailing the progress of the disease. The milieu is vividly and realistically depicted. Perhaps Hesse's preoccupation with the perspective of the painter helped towards attainment of this visual clarity which contrasts with the more amorphous musicality of *Gertrud.*

The plot and the network of problems reveal no loose ends. All is tightly interwoven: the several paintings of Veraguth whose composition we witness are all connected with the family situation and the artist's problem. In the last picture, little Pierre stands between his divided parents:

> There were three life-size figures: a man and a woman, each sunk in himself and lost to the other, and between them a child playing, in peaceful gaiety unconscious of the cloud pressing down above him. . . . He painted this child with all the charm and nobility of his best portraits; the figures at either side sat in petrified sym-

metry, rigorous suffering images of isolation—the man with his head supported in his hand engrossed in melancholy brooding, the woman lost in suffering and empty dullness. (II, 536)

But, ironically, while the painter projects into this picture both his unhappy marital situation and his love for his little son, his engrossment in the creative act removes him from real contact with Pierre. On the next page we read that during these days of absorption in his work, "if the boy crossed his path, he would kiss him on the brow while lost in thought,would look into his eyes with a sad absent-mindedness and go on his way." Encouraged by his father to come to him at any time, even when he is at work, Pierre replies:

"You know, Papa, when I visit you in the studio, you always pat my head and say nothing and your eyes are quite different and sometimes full of anger. And if one says anything, one can see from your eyes that you aren't listening, you just say 'indeed' and pay no attention. And if I come to you and want to tell you something, then I want you to listen!" (II, 542)

Not only the picture symbolizes the artist's dilemma in his marriage and the effort to win his son, but Pierre's long final illness and his death can also be seen as symbolic representations of the basic theme.

In the early stage of his illness, Pierre has a dream which foreshadows his own fate and symbolizes the basic themes. Wandering in the gardens, he comes across his father, his mother, and his brother, but these figures pass without awareness of him or of each other. He wants to call to them but something hinders him: "He had no real will to do so." He comes to a small pond, from which his narcissistic image peers at him—but his face is like the others, "old and pale and firmly fixed in indifferent rigor." Again his father approaches, and he tries to call. Although no sound comes forth, the father turns around and sees him:

He looked at him closely with his searching painter's gaze, smiled faintly, and nodded slightly, kindly and sympathetically, but without comfort, as if nothing could be done to help. For a brief moment a shadow of love and related suffering passed across his stern face, and in this brief moment he was no longer the strong father but rather a poor helpless brother. (II, 573)

As Hesse himself observed, *Rosshalde* has withstood the test of time far better than any of his other prewar writings. Its controlled realism and conciseness, the absence of specifically German or Romantic elements, the marital theme and, above all, the moving experience of the child's vision and his inner and outer world, culminating in his agony—all these factors suggest that even today this work ought to appeal to the English-reading public. It is all the more surprising that this is the only longer work of Hesse not so far available in English! *Gertrud,*[6] the first novel to be translated into English, on the other hand, is the least satisfactory and the least likely to appeal to the modern English reader. Thus it can be said that, from the beginning, Hesse's path towards recognition in the English-speaking world was beset by bad judgment and bad translations.[7]

CHAPTER 4

Demian and Symbols of Transformation

I Krieg und Frieden

THIS phrase, the title of one of the pieces, was later chosen by Hesse for his collection of wartime essays,[1] the first of which, "O Freunde nicht diese Töne," was published on November 3, 1914, in the *Neue Zürcher Zeitung*. One of the changes brought about by the war is thus a growing concern, on the author's part, with wider social and political problems. Hesse's prewar writings had tended toward preoccupation with the individual and his inner life and in this respect, they are representative of the tendency of the *Bildungsroman* and of the Romantic tradition, with its stress on subjectivity and inwardness. These qualities are marked in *Knulp* (*Three Stories from Knulp's Life*), which was published in 1915 but written entirely before the war. Indeed, the first story had been published as early as 1908 in *Die neue Rundschau*. *Knulp* enjoyed considerable success, but today its charm is seen to lie almost wholly in its gentle evocation of an amiable outsider in the manner of Eichendorff's homeless wanderer *Taugenichts*. But Hesse's typically German apolitical attitude before 1914 has to be qualified. Although his own contributions made few references to social and political problems, nevertheless he was co-editor of *März*, a journal noted for its opposition to Emperor William II. Indeed the title of this publication makes obvious reference to the "March days" of the Revolution of 1848. *Simplicissimus,* for which Hesse also wrote, had attained wider notoriety for its anti-government political barbs.

The title of Hesse's first wartime essay evoked the words of Schiller and the music of Beethoven to protest against the war as a "taking back" of Beethoven's Ninth Symphony with its call to brotherly love—"seid umschlungen, Millionen!"—just as Mann's Leverkühn, with his *Dr. Fausti Weheklag,* composes an anti-Beethoven work cunningly inserting pessimism in place of Beethoven's soaring optimism.

This appeal to humanity for humaneness brought Hesse an immediate answer from Romain Rolland, whose work before the war had been aimed at Franco-German understanding and amity, especially in the novel *Jean Christophe.* The friendship thus formed continued through the years, until Rolland's last communication to Hesse was returned by the Vichy censor in 1940. The correspondence has been handsomely printed and adorned with watercolors by Hesse.[2] Rolland's letters are given in the original French and Hesse's replies in German.

For Hesse the repercussions of his anti-war stand were drastic, and in "Kurzgefasster Lebenslauf" (1926) he gave an ironic picture of former friends and admirers turning away from him:

The consequence . . . was, that in the press of my fatherland I was declared a traitor. . . . Of all my friends—and I thought I had many in the press—only two ventured to stand up for me. Old friends gave me to understand that they had been nourishing a viper in their bosoms, and that these bosoms in future would beat only for *Kaiser* and *Reich* but no longer for degenerate me. (IV, 476–77)

Meanwhile, having moved from Gaienhofen to Berne, in 1912, Hesse was a German citizen resident in Switzerland. Feeling as he did about the war, he could not participate as a belligerent, but he also did not stand aloof: he offered his services in humanitarian work for the relief of prisoners and internees in Switzerland and, in this capacity, was loosely connected with the German Embassy in the federal capital of Berne. His main task was to provide reading material, and this led to his founding of the *Interniertenzeitung*, which he edited and for which he wrote.

As the war dragged on for months and years, Hesse suffered increasingly under the strain, which was aggravated by a deepening domestic crisis. The prolonged illness of his youngest son, Martin, with cerebral meningitis occurred in the first year of the war. His father died in 1916, and Hesse made the sad trip home to Germany for the funeral. Meanwhile his wife's mental condition deteriorated and in 1918 she had to be confined to an institution.

At this low point in his life, Hesse met the brilliant young psychiatrist Dr. J. B. Lang, a disciple of C. G. Jung, and in 1916–17 he underwent a sequence of seventy-two psychoanalytic sittings in Lucerne. It would be a mistake to assume, however, that Hesse had suffered a complete nervous breakdown. Like many creative artists, Hesse had a sensitive personality with a neurotic tendency. During the months of consultation with Dr. Lang, he continued to write, and the reviews and letters of this period testify to his retention of full mental power. But he may well have been nearing the point of nervous instability. It is likely, however, that he continued the sessions with Dr. Lang more because of the warm friendship between the two men and an insatiable interest in psychoanalysis which had already manifested itself in his reviews of psychoanalytical works.

According to Hugo Ball, *Demian* was written in white heat, under the immediate impact of the psychotherapy of Dr. Lang, who appears in the book in the guise of Pistorius. Dr. Lang also reappears in other writings, including *Die Morgenlandfahrt*, under the name Longus. The connection with Jung is clear but the Romantic tradition, too, involves a probing of the unconscious. The novel appeared in 1919 under the pseudonym Emil Sinclair and with the title *Demian, The Story of a Youth;* it was at once hailed as an important work. The award of the Fontane Prize forced Hesse to reveal his identity, since this prize was tenable only by new writers. To the German reader the name Sinclair may well have suggested the work's Romantic affinity through association with Hölderlin. Before probing the Jungian ties, we shall examine other levels of interpretation.

II Bildungsroman

On one level *Demian* falls into the pattern of the *Bildungsroman* which has dominated the form of the German novel from the Romantics to Thomas Mann. We are introduced to the hero, Emil Sinclair, as a boy innocent of the world: a veritable *tabula rasa*. Like other writers in this genre, Hesse portrays many autobiographical elements not only in the external environment of the boy Emil, his pious family, and the small town in which he is brought up but also, as we shall see, in the deeper psychological development which Hesse experienced.

As in the *Bildungsroman*, we follow the development of the callow youth guided by a wise mentor, Demian, through a variety of experiences. This Eden-like innocence is disturbed by the intrusion of Kromer who sees through the child's boastful lie about stealing the apples and uses this knowledge as a form of blackmail to wield demonic power over Sinclair. Out of the blue, a new boy in school, Demian, divines the nature of Kromer's influence and liberates Sinclair from it.

Instead of seeking out his liberator, Sinclair retreats like the prodigal son to his mother's apron strings, trying to pretend that all is as before. But later he is brought together with Demian in the confirmation class. Sinclair's unthinking acceptance of the conventional teaching is jolted by Demian's gnostic interpretation of the story of Cain and Abel, seeing in Cain, the marked man, the exceptional exponent of genius who became the victim of jealousy on the part of the less endowed envious members of the human family.

The confirmation classes coincide with awakening sexuality and disturbing dreams. These are more Jungian than Freudian in character, with the exception of one which suggests the Oedipus complex when Sinclair's enemy Kromer forces him into a murderous attack on his father.

Chapter Three, entitled "Der Schächer" ("Thief on the Cross"), features Demian's apparently perverse praise of the thief who was crucified with Christ and did not repent. This leads Demian to declare that one would have to create for oneself a God who includes the Devil within himself, thereby anticipating Abraxas. Sinclair has thus been stimulated to question conventional patterns of thought and behavior as his "child-hood fell in ruins about him." Demian and his mother move away and Sinclair goes to St (Stuttgart) to study at the *Gymnasium*.

With the fourth chapter, "Beatrice," we are halfway through the novel. Sinclair's feeling of isolation and emptiness is succeeded by a period of dissipation, from which he is saved by the sight of a girl whom he never meets but whom he names Beatrice and worships from afar. His life has suddenly been' converted, like St. Paul's, from depravity to austerity. He dreams of Beatrice and begins to paint, in the attempt to give form to his ideal. His attempts to realize this vision result in a hermaphroditic countenance resembling Demian. He dreams of Demian and then of a bird fighting its way out of the egg. He rises to paint this vision and sends the picture to Demian, even though he no longer knows the latter's address. At the beginning of the next chapter, he mysteriously finds on his desk in the classroom an enigmatic answer from Demian.

In the Greek class, Sinclair awakens from his revery to hear the teacher commenting on the nature of Abraxas, "a divinity with the symbolic task of uniting the divine and the diabolical." Although there is no sudden break or change in style and narrative technique, at this point—halfway through the text—we become increasingly aware of a blurring of external reality and of an increasing emphasis on Sinclair's inner psychological world. We tend to ask whether Demian, Frau Eva, and Beatrice have any "real" existence outside of Sinclair's mind—or rather his unconscious.

Looked at as a whole, the novel shows a remarkable development. At the beginning, we feel comfortably secure in the familiar narrative technique, which delineates the boy Sinclair in a clearly outlined external environment. But imperceptibly, the persons and things surrounding Sinclair retreat into a shadowy unreality which exists only for the sake of Sinclair and especially his unconscious. This divergence from the usual pattern of the *Bildungsroman* becomes clear when one compares it, for example, with Thomas Mann's *Der Zauberberg*, in which Mann, too, is concerned primarily with the inner psyche of Hans Castorp. Here, too, there is a preponderance of abstraction, philosophic discussions, and dreams. But all this takes place in a clearly defined social and physical milieu. Hesse has gone further in that the very form and technique of his novel symbolize the progressive penetration in depth of the hero's unconscious.

III   C. G. Jung and the Symbols

Ziolkowski,[3] Dahrendorf[4] and Boulby[5] have explored the relationship of *Demian* to Jung but without, it seems to me, exhausting all its implications. Ziolkowski, for instance, discusses the influence of Christianity, of Bachofen, Schopenhauer, and Nietzsche as well as that of Jung. It is obvious, of course, that in Hesse's early life Christianity was a powerful factor. It is equally obvious that he had read Nietzsche, just as it is probable that he was familiar with the ideas of Bachofen which were, at this time, "rediscovered" largely through the work of C. A. Bernoulli (1868–1937).

On the other hand, we know not only of Hesse's indirect knowledge of Jung through Dr. Lang (through whom they became personally acquainted), but we now have Hesse's own admission of his knowledge of Jung and especially his *Symbols of Transformation*.[6] In this work, first published in 1912, ideas and symbols of Christianity, of Bachofen, of Nietzsche and Schopenhauer figure significantly. It seems likely, then, that for *Demian* at least, all the other influences are transmuted through Jung.

In this connection, it is well to note that, for Jung, symbols are not explicit; they are not "signs" that stand for specific "things" but rather suggestive analogies. In Jung's words: "A symbol is an indefinite expression with many meanings, pointing to something not easily defined and therefore not fully known. . . . The symbol therefore has a large number of analogous variants."[7]

This passage suggests that we must be cautious in relating symbols to explicit concepts. For two generations, *Demian* has exercised a spell over many readers, most of whom, it is safe to say, were unaware of the Jungian overtones. These readers, nevertheless, must have intuitively sensed the general tendency of the symbols and the probing of the psyche in them. But if a knowledge of Jung is not necessary, it may still be helpful to the reader of *Demian*.

Jung differs from Freud in his concept of the libido, which Jung conceives as "psychic energy," of which sexuality is only one of many channels. The attraction to the mother and the incest prohibition, which are conceived in sexual terms by Freud, are related by Jung to symbols rather than to the objects themselves, and these symbols play an important role in the development of the individual toward maturity, and of the culture of society as a whole. Jung pours scorn on Freud's term "subconscious" as implying something lower. For all we know it may be higher, and he, therefore, uses the term "unconscious." Furthermore, Jung posits the existence of a racial or collective unconscious which transcends the individual's unconscious, and in which the individual shares. In Jung's words, "it was manifestly not a question of inherited ideas, but of an inborn disposition to produce parallel images, or rather of identical psychic structures common to all men, which I later called the archetypes of the collective unconscious" (p. 158).

The way in which a work like *Demian* makes its impact upon the innocent reader who has not taken a course in psychology seems implicit in Jung's statement:

> [The] creative fantasy is continually engaged in producing analogies to instinctual processes in order to free the libido from sheer instinctuality by guiding it towards analogous ideas. . . . Their special character is, I believe, to be discerned in the fact that they are archetypes, that is, universal and inherited patterns which, taken together, constitute the structure of the unconscious. (pp. 227-28)

The theme of *Demian* might be described in simplest terms as "know thyself"—a dictum at least as old as Socrates. But Hesse gives a radically new twist in interpreting this as an injunction to penetrate to the depths of the unconscious. Furthermore, Hesse goes beyond mere knowledge for its own sake to posit action in the tradition of Faust's declaration: "Im Anfang war die Tat."

This progress to self-knowledge and the new morality takes place in a triadic rhythm which is common to such widely divergent doctrines as Christian theology, eighteenth-century idealism, and Jungian psychology. The Christian moves from original innocence in Eden through the Fall from Grace, ensuing sin, sacrifice, and atonement to redemption in Heaven. Schiller's triadic pattern traced at the end of the eighteenth century, embraces a first stage of unconscious harmony of instinct and law in "pure nature," followed by a second stage (*Kulturzustand*), characterized by disharmony and conflict between "duty" (*Pflicht*) and "inclination" (*Neigung*) in which one should strive to reach the third and ultimate stage (*das Ideal*) in which harmony is to be restored, but on a conscious basis. Hesse's most explicit formulation—for which he expressly disclaims originality—is found in "Ein Stückchen Theologie" ("A Little Bit of Theology," 1932):

The path of human development begins with innocence (paradise, childhood, irresponsible preparatory stage). From there it leads into guilt, into the knowledge of good and evil, into the demands of *Kultur* [civilized society—in the same essay Hesse refers to Freud's *Unbehagen in der Kultur*], morality, religions, and ideals of humanity. In everyone who lives through this stage seriously and as a differentiated individual it ends irrevocably in despair, namely in the insight that there is no possibility of realizing virtue, of perfect obedience, of a satisfying service, that justice is unattainable. Now this despair leads either to destruction or to a Third Kingdom of *Geist*, to experiencing a condition beyond ethics and law, a penetration to grace and redemption, to a new and higher kind of irresponsibility, or briefly expressed: to faith. (VII, 389)

This pattern of thought will be seen to underlie Hesse's remaining works, but especially *Der Steppenwolf* and *Die Morgenlandfahrt*.

Jung sees all higher achievements (all culture) dependent upon channeling the libido (i.e. psychic energy) into symbolic analogies of basic instinctual trends. Thus the child is attracted to its mother:

But what was natural and useful to the child is a psychic danger for the adult, and this is expressed by the symbol of incest. Because the incest taboo opposes the libido and blocks the path of regression, it is possible for the libido to be canalized into the mother analogies thrown up by the unconscious. In that way, the libido becomes progessive again and even attains a higher level of consciousness than before. (p. 213)

Many of the symbols which later develop and expand like leitmotifs are subtly implanted in the early stages of the story, while the reader may be under the illusion that he is dealing with a straightforward realistic narrative. On the first page, we are introduced to the polarity of the world: "Two worlds clashed there, from two poles came night and day." The "good" world is that of parents, orthodox Christianity, bourgeois standards; the "evil" world is criminality, sex, slaughterhouse, death, drunkenness. In a larger sense, this could imply the impingement of the outside world, and especially the First World War, upon the protected individual. In any case, it impinges upon Sinclair in the form of Franz Kromer, the emissary from the evil world outside. This prepares us for the later development of the polarity in the symbol of the all-inclusive deity Abraxas.

Sinclair's father reproaches him for wearing wet shoes, and this engenders in the son a feeling of superiority over the father and is the first step towards his liberation from the protected world of childhood: "it was a first dint in the pillars on which my childhood had rested and which everybody must have destroyed, before he can become himself" (III, 115). Thus early is adumbrated the theme of the necessity of standing alone without pillars or props, and we are prepared for the development beyond Demian and Frau Eva at the end of the book.

In the second chapter, arriving to rescue his friend from the clutches of Kromer, Demian draws Sinclair's attention to the bird in relief on the lintel of the Sinclair dwelling and introduces the Cain-motif—the mark being a distinction (*Zeichen*= *Auszeichnung*). But Sinclair's reaction is to avoid Demian and retreat to his mother—expressed in language highly suggestive of psychoanalytic usage: "I retreated to the lap [*Schoss*=lap, womb] of my mother and to the security of a protected, pious, childlike innocence. I made myself younger, more dependent, more childlike than I was . . . for I was not yet capable of walking alone" (III, 141). This, in Jungian concepts, is infantile regression which has not become productive by transference to symbolic analogies: "When a person remains bound to the mother, the life he ought to have lived runs away in the form of conscious and unconscious fantasies" (p. 307). Thus Sinclair lived increasingly in dream fantasies: "What I experienced in these dreams and what I experienced in reality I can no longer clearly separate" (III, 130). This passage contains one of increasingly frequent hints tending away from the everyday reality towards symbolic fantasy.

Young Sinclair's retreat "into the lost paradise that was reopening" (III, 140), his reception as the "returning prodigal son," cast an ambivalent and ironic light on the relationship of good and evil. For the "good" world is "bad" for the boy, inhibiting his development toward independence and responsibility (in Jungian terms). This is the more striking in its use of Christian imagery in the passages above and is suggestive of Nietzsche's anti-Christian "Umwertung aller Werte" in Demian's words: "Therefore each of us has to find out for himself what is permitted and what is forbidden—forbidden to *him*" (III, 158).

With the beginning of the third chapter, "Der Schächer," the narrator hints again at the increasing inwardness of the action: "But I am interested only in the steps I took in my life to arrive at myself." The bird-symbol re-enters as Sinclair sees Demian sketching the stone relief over his door. Turning away from the dying horse in the street, Sinclair sees Demian's face, which is a boy's face but also a man's and again "it was as if something of a female countenance was in it" (III, 146).

In the chapter entitled "Symbols of the Mother and of Rebirth," Jung declares: "Just as the female lies hidden in the male, so the male lies hidden in the female" (p. 221), and again "we recognize the typical elements of a libido myth: original bisexuality, immortality . . . through entry into the mother . . . resurrection as a soul-bird" (p. 289). Thus the gossip that Demian lived in incest with his mother (III, 147) is not to be taken literally but symbolically, just as are later suggestions of sexual attraction in Sinclair's attitude to Frau Eva. This is stated explicitly by Jung:

It must be remembered that the "mother" is really an imago, a psychic image merely. . . . The "mother," as the first incarnation of the anima archetype, personifies in fact the whole unconscious. Hence the regression leads back only apparently to the mother; in reality she is the gateway into the unconscious, into the "realm of the Mothers." (p. 330)

Demian's re-evaluation of the thief on the cross who died unrepentant is related to Cain. As Demian remarks, "He is a character, and people of character always come off badly in Biblical history. Perhaps he is also a descendant of Cain. Don't you think so?" (III, 156). This is followed by the admonition to create for oneself a God "who also includes within himself the devil." Stimulated by Demian in this way, Sinclair suddenly sees and feels, "how deeply my most individual personal life and thought participated in the eternal flux of great ideas" (III, 157)—a clear reference to Jung's collective unconscious and its archetypes.

At the beginning of the "Beatrice" chapter, Sinclair sinks into the sin of sloth and drunkenness while away from home attending the *Gymnasium* in Stuttgart. The motif "through sin to sainthood" resounds strongly in the Dostoyevsky essays which followed *Demian*. It is not even clear whether there is a great deal of overt misbehavior since reality is receding and the dream world, or rather the unconscious, is looming more in the foreground of the novel: "It was like a bad dream. I see myself, a spellbound dreamer, crawling restlessly in torment through sticky dirt" (III, 170).

In any case—real in the literal sense or real in the psychoanalytic sense—Sinclair senses his sinful path is a stage on the way to salvation: "There are many ways in which God can isolate us and lead us to ourselves." Beyond the reference to Dostoyevsky, this can clearly be interpreted in the sense in which the regressive instinctual urges, according to Jung, must be redirected to symbolic analogies. Sinclair finds his libido (i.e. psychic energy) concentrated upon a beautiful unknown girl, whom he names Beatrice and whom he worships. The reference to Dante's idealized figure is obvious, but according to Jung: "The variety of forms in which the soul-image may appear is well-nigh inexhaustible. . . . The anima can equally well take the form of a sweet young maiden . . . typical anima figures in literature are Helen of Troy . . . Beatrice in the Divine Comedy. . . ."[8]

Sinclair, having suddenly abandoned the sinful life, is now regarded as a saint among his fellows and is entreated by a younger pupil, Knauer, for help. Sinclair feels helpless, for this is a process that must be accomplished within the individual's unconscious. Nevertheless, mysteriously attracted at the critical moment, Sinclair does save Knauer from suicide.

Sinclair dreams of Demian and the bird in the heraldic emblem which Demian forces him to eat. Having eaten, Sinclair feels the swallowed bird alive within him and awakes. The next day he paints the bird: "Now it was a bird of prey with a sharp bold sparrow-hawk's head. Half its body was still stuck in a dark cosmic sphere, out of which it was working its way as out of a gigantic egg" (III, 183). Demian provides the following interpretation: "The bird is fighting its way out of the egg. The egg is the world. Whoever will be born again must destroy a world. The bird is flying to God. The God is called Abraxas" (III, 185).

This laconic statement combines a number of motifs about which Jung has written:

The world is enclosed in the egg which surrounds it on all sides; it is the cosmic birth-giver, a symbol used by Plato and by the Vedas. This "mother" is omnipresent, like the air. But air is spirit, so the world-mother is a spirit, the anima mundi. The hieroglyph is at the same time a quaternity-symbol, which psychologically always points to the self. It therefore depicts the uttermost circumference and the innermost centre. (p. 354)

Moreover, birds are helpful animals "who represent the stirrings or intuitions of the unconscious, the helpful mother" (p. 352). But Hesse's symbol of the bird breaking its way out of the egg is of a syncretic nature, apparently transcending Jung's analyses and combining with other symbols: the necessity of destroying in order to be reborn, hence an allusion to the path to virtue through depravity. The reborn soul is on the way to discovering the personal God who combines the polarities of "good" and "evil."

Sinclair now is drawn to the young organist, Pistorius, a renegade student of theology. Hugo Ball and others have claimed that Hesse has portrayed in Pistorius his psychoanalyst Dr. Lang. This is certainly correct in that Pistorius has the effect on Sinclair of a psychoanalytic therapist. He encourages meditation, reveries, the communication of inmost thoughts and dreams, and he is preeminently interested in primitive myths and symbols, as was Dr. Lang. But the figure of Pistorius is no portrait of the Lucerne doctor, and certain divergences are striking. Pistorius is, above all, a musician, and music brings Sinclair and Pistorius together, forming the background of their meditation and penetration to the unconscious. Dr. Lang is said to have been markedly unmusical but to have had a lively interest in painting. As a matter of fact, Hesse's career as a painter dates from his friendship with Dr. Lang. On the other hand, music, no doubt, seemed to Hesse to have a more direct relationship with the unconscious. Sinclair says to Pistorius:

I like to listen to music but only the kind you play, absolute music, music in which one feels that a human being is shaking heaven and hell. I am very fond of music, I think because it has so little to do with morality. (III, 194)

In the two chapters that cover Sinclair's friendship with Pistorius, the main themes and symbols re-enter and acquire additional leitmotif allusions: Abraxas—the necessity of including evil as well as good—the bird and the egg, the references to the Gnostics, and to the collective unconscious, which is clearly suggested in Pistorius' explanation:

We always draw the boundaries of our personality much too close. . . . We consist of all the constituents of the world, each of us, and just as our body bears in itself the genealogical tables of development back to the fish and much farther still, so we have in our psyche everything that has ever existed in the human soul. All gods and devils that have ever been . . . are in us, as potentialities, wishes, outlets. If mankind were obliterated except for a modestly gifted child . . . this child would rediscover the whole course of events, would be able to reproduce everything, gods, demons, paradises, commandments, prohibitions, old and new testaments. (III, 199)

If this is the case, Sinclair asks, what then is the role of the individual? In his answer, Pistorius points directly to the psychoanalytic function: the aim of raising the unconscious to the conscious, to master and possess it. A madman can produce thoughts reminiscent of Plato, he says; a small boy in a Moravian settlement can think deep mythological sequences that occur among the Gnostics or in Zoroaster, but without being aware of all this. Only when the first flash of cognition dawns does he become a human being. Pistorius continues in a vein suggestive of Hesse's later humor:

After all, you surely won't regard all bipeds running around the street as human beings, merely because they walk upright and gestate their young nine months? See how many of them are fish or sheep, worms or leeches, how many ants, how many bees! In each of them, the human potentialities are present, but only in so far as he is intuitively aware of them and learns to raise them into consciousness, do these potentialities belong to him. (III, 200)

Jacob's struggle with the angel, which is the heading of the second of the Pistorius chapters, is discussed by C. G. Jung in the course of his long disquisition on Longfellow's *Hiawatha:*

It is not a man who is transformed into a god, but the god who undergoes transformation in and through man. . . . Consequently he appears at first in ,hostile form, as an assailant with whom the hero has to wrestle. . . . The struggle has its parallel in Jacob's wrestling with the angel at the ford Jabbok. The onslaught of instinct then becomes an experience of divinity, provided that man does not succumb to it and follow it blindly, but defends his humanity against the animal nature of the divine power. (pp. 337-38)

This exemplifies the close-knit texture of symbols and motifs, for the struggle of Jacob with the angel is relative to the struggle to penetrate the unconscious and also to the Abraxas symbol relating to the amoral unity of good and evil. Jacob's struggle also leads directly to Sinclair's inner struggle against Pistorius, who has been a guardian angel to him; and the inevitable wound he inflicts in breaking with Pistorius conjures up the Cain symbol again: "It was then that I first became aware of the mark of Cain on my brow."

But in the triadic rhythm this involvement in guilt is a necessary step on the road to self-knowledge and progress: "The true vocation for everyone was simply to arrive at oneself." This realization of the true ideal leads to isolation which conjures up Jesus in Gethsemane and on the cross—re-evoking the gnostic interpretation of the thief on the cross.

Whoever really wills nothing but his fate has no longer his like but stands entirely alone and has only cold cosmic space around him. You know, that is Jesus in the Garden of Gethsemane. (III, 222)

This absolute isolation of the awakened individual is also strongly reminiscent of Nietzsche: "You isolated individuals of today shall be a Chosen People. . . . Seek solitude, in order to benefit many." [9] If, in one sense, Pistorius represents the Jungian psychoanalyst who encourages meditation, dreaming and thinking in symbols, in another sense one can see him as a representative of Romanticism pointing to the past. Sinclair realizes this: "His ideal was 'antiquarian,' his quest was regressive, he was a Romantic" (III, 218). On the autobiographical level, we glimpse Hesse's transcendence of his early Romantic orientation. But it is not an abrogation of Romanticism, for Hesse-Sinclair is fully aware of the debt owed to this movement, which even provides the means to transcend it, for he realizes that Pistorius "had led me along a path destined to transcend him and abandon him" (III, 218).

On parting from Pistorius, Sinclair has found the road—the path to the unconscious—but has not yet liberated it and freed himself:

Ich war ein Wurf der Natur, ein Wurf ins Ungewisse, vielleicht zu Neuem, vielleicht zu Nichts, und diesen Wurf aus der Urtiefe auswirken zu lassen, seinen Willen in mir zu fühlen und ihn ganz zu meinem zu machen, das allein war mein Beruf.[10]

In the next chapter, he confronts Frau Eva, whose name suggests her character in the novel as a Jungian symbol of the *Urmutter*: "She was my dream image . . . *Dämon* and mother. my fate and my beloved" (III, 223–224). As Jung puts it:

The task consists in integrating the unconscious, in bringing together "conscious" and "unconscious." I have called this the individuation process, . . . "Entry into the mother" then means establishing a relationship between the ego and the unconscious. Nietzsche probably means something of the kind in his poem, "Between Birds of Prey." (p. 301)

The network of symbols becomes more integrated. Sinclair "lives with Nietzsche," feeling the isolation of his soul, as others seek "warm herd proximity." The mark of Cain distinguishes *both* Demian and Sinclair. The picture of the yellow bird with the hawk's head forcing itself out of the egg is prominent in Demian's home. Frau Eva bears the distinguishing mark of Cain as well. She is "like the mother of all beings." The outside world has dissolved into an inner kaleidoscopic world of the unconscious: "But here within was love and spiritual life, here lived the fairy tale and the dream" (III, 236). The hints of eros, of incest even, are dissolved into pure symbols, as a transference of libido, in Jung's sense:

My love for Frau Eva seemed the only content of my life. But every day she looked different. Often I had the feeling that it was not her person toward which my being strove, but that she was only a symbol of my inner psyche—endeavoring to lead me only deeper into myself. Often I heard words from her which sounded like answers of my unconscious to burning questions stirring within me. (III, 242)

Sinclair's vision of his yellow bird soaring heavenward out of the sultry storm clouds heralds the approach and outbreak of the Great War, which is real enough despite the psychological inwardness of the latter part of the novel. But Demian's presence on a stretcher beside Sinclair in the field hospital is manifestly a vision, and his disappearance is symbolic of Sinclair's goal in coming to terms with his own unconscious.

IV   The Individual and Society

With all its veiling of concrete reality in favor of psychological "inwardness," *Demian* expands to embrace European society on the eve of the Great War. This increasing concern with the supra-personal in the latter portion of the book runs counter to the symbolic retreat from the outer world to the inner recesses of the unconscious in the individual. But here, too, Jung had prepared the way with his doctrine of the collective unconscious. The picture Hesse gives is of Western civilization sick with repression and frustration, refusing to acknowledge the source of active progress in the creative myths of the collective unconscious. Nietzsche's doctrine of herd morality is implicit, and the rising *Angst* springs from lack of inner harmony through denying the well-springs in the unconscious. Demian makes this explicit when he states: "But it concerns not me alone, . . . I distinguish rather precisely those dreams that indicate stirrings in my own soul and the other infrequent ones in which the whole fate of man is indicated" (III, 247).

The novel is therefore related to others diagnosing the rottenness of European society on the eve of World War I, such as Thomas Mann's *Der Zauberberg*, Musil's *Der Mann ohne Eigenschaften*, and Joseph Roth's *Radetzkymarsch;* and the symbol of the bird expands from the individual to embrace the collective fate of Western Europe and to herald the outbreak of war:

There came driven across the heavens a slack yellow cloud. It was blocked by the gray wall and the wind quickly formed from the yellow and the blue an image, a huge bird which tore itself loose from the blue chaos and with broad beats of its wings disappeared into the heavens. Then the storm became audible and rain rattled down mixed with hail. An abrupt crash of thunder, sounding improbable and frightening, descended upon the lashed countryside. Immediately afterwards, a ray of sunlight burst through, and on the near mountains above the brown forest the pale snow gave off a pallid unreal phosphorescence. (III, 245)

In this image, the violence of the storm is mitigated by the phoenix-like attributes of the bird which rises into Heaven, so that the impression is optimistic. The reader feels that the pain and suffering of humanity presage a rebirth: "The world is bent on renewal. There is a smell of death. Nothing new comes without death" (III, 247).

Hesse expressed this feeling in his analysis of Dostoyevsky's *Brothers Karamazov* (1919) when he stated: "This decline is a return to the Mother, it is a return to Asia, to the sources, to the Faustian 'Mothers' and it will, of course, like every death on earth lead to a new birth" (VII, 162). The meaning implicit in *Demian* is also expressed in Hesse's lines on Dostoyevsky's *Idiot:* "The future is uncertain, but the way which is indicated here is unambiguous. It signifies new psychic orientation" (VII, 185).

This message had a tonic effect upon two generations of young Germans hopeless in defeat amid the ruins not merely of the physical environment but of the ideals which they had taken over and accepted unthinkingly and uncritically. The tendency to look elsewhere for the blame is countered by Hesse's admonition to examine and purge the unconscious:

The primitive urges, even the wildest, were not aimed at the enemy. Their bloody work was only the emanation of the interior, of the psyche divided in itself, which was intent on raging and killing, destroying and dying, in order to be able to be born again. (III, 254)

In the ending, the rebirth of Sinclair becomes almost explicit through the veiled dreamlike atmosphere of the military hospital. Demian on the next stretcher disappears after saying to Sinclair: "Then you will have to harken to the voice within and you will perceive that I am deep inside you." And as his wounds are bandaged, Sinclair finds the "key" through the pain: "When I . . . descend deep into myself, where in the dark mirror the images of fate slumber, then . . . I see my own image which now entirely resembles Him, my friend and guide."

The capitalization of this last pronoun is the last of many pieces of evidence adduced by Ziolkowski to support his contention that Demian is a Christ figure: "He disputes with his teachers, preaches a coming kingdom, and instructs his band of disciples through parables." [11] In view of other evidence it is probably irrelevant to ask whether Demian has a "band of disciples" or only one, for the other figures near the end are mere shadows.

Ziolkowski goes on to qualify his contention by referring to Nietzsche, pointing out the irony in "an essentially Nietzschean doctrine . . . promulgated in a novel whose structure, language, images, and impulses are basically religious." He refers to Pistorius' statement that he regarded Christ "not as a deity but as a myth, a *heros*, as an image that mankind has painted on the walls of eternity." He then adds: "Pistorius reveals himself by these remarks an heir of the theological tradition of Strauss, Renan, and Feuerbach." This statement points away from Jung, who is represented directly in the Pistorius–Dr. Lang figure, and it is Jung himself who clarifies the sense in which Demian can be viewed as a Christ figure:

Christ, as a hero and god-man, signifies psychologically the self: that is he represents the projection of this most important and most central of archetypes; the archetype of the self has, functionally, the significance of a ruler of the inner world, i.e. of the collective unconscious. The self, as a symbol of wholeness is a *coincidentia oppositorum*, and therefore contains light and darkness simultaneously. (p. 368)

In this limited Jungian sense, Demian can be seen as a Christ figure simultaneously gathering into itself the individual and collective unconscious and the wholeness that is comprised of the opposites good and evil, light and dark.

Are Demian and Frau Eva mere symbols, or do they also exist as real characters? On one level, of course, they do. No doubt the book has been so read by a multitude of readers. In this case, the story must have the appeal of Romantic mystery since so much pertaining to these figures is veiled, mystical, and beyond ordinary logic and comprehension. We have already seen how the at first more or less sharply etched lines of outer reality become progressively blurred as the novel moves relentlessly inward toward the unconscious. This process can be followed in the figure of Demian up to his final submergence in Sinclair as his daemon.

Jung's analysis of Longfellow's poem applies equally well to Sinclair:

Hiawatha has in himself the possibility, indeed the necessity, of confronting his daemon. On the way to this goal he conquers the parents and breaks the infantile ties. But the deepest tie is to the mother. Once he has conquered this by gaining access to her symbolic equivalent, he can be born again. In this tie to the maternal source lies the strength that gives the hero his extraordinary powers, his true genius, which he frees from the embrace of the unconscious by his daring and sovereign independence. Thus the god is born in him. (p. 336)

This suggests that in Sinclair there is an element of the artist figure, never far from the works of Hesse. He paints, he is in a high degree responsive to music—and the highly charged poetic prose of the novel (written in the first person) is, according to the fiction, his own creation. He explores the unconscious and, absorbing Demian, becomes himself the "marked" man. And there are also the autobiographical allusions to the poet Hesse, mentioned earlier. It is, therefore, not as improbable as Ziolkowski asserts that the name Sinclair was intended by Hesse as a tribute to Hölderlin's friend Isaak von Sinclair. Indeed Jung's *Symbols of Transformation* deals extensively with Hölderlin. Isaak von Sinclair tried and failed to be Hölderlin's daemon in order to prevent him from succumbing to madness. Hesse has esoterically and ironically altered the relationship, for in his book Demian tries and succeeds in befriending Sinclair, saving him and raising him to the possibility of rebirth and poetic productivity. J. C. Middleton's reading of the name Sinclair, whether or not it was intended by Hesse, is valid in shedding interpretative light, for he sees it as an Anglo-French compound of "sin" and "clair"—of the two worlds of the novel, the "dark" and the "light." [12]

In an interesting discussion of other names[13] occurring in the
book Joseph Mileck has suggested that Emil may be a link with
the *Bildungsroman* of Rousseau or the valiant Roman Scipio
Emilianus, while Max may point to the superlative implications
(Maximus) inherent in Demian. Pistorius is more suitable for
a student of mythology than its German equivalent Bäcker. It
is not improbable that Hesse may have known of the sixteenth-
century church dignitary in Baden, Johann Pistorius, who likewise was the son of a pastor. The frail, helpless Knauer, ob-
sessed by the evil and filth of sex, is a whimperer, as the name
suggests by analogy with *kauern* (to cower). Frau Eva is both
what the Hebrew word implies (life, living) and what the name
has come to symbolize: the mythical mother of mankind, especially as conceived by Jung as the *anima mundi*.

The novel *Demian* towers as a landmark in the career and
inner development of Hesse, from whose tortured soul the work
proceeded. The author's indebtedness to Jung in no sense invali-
dates his inventive genius. His novel exists on a separate plane
from psychoanalytic doctrines and yet, at the same time, it is one
of the most striking literary manifestations provoked and stimulated by modern psychoanalysis. With all this, and with its radi-
cal moral doctrine, the work affirms the enduring legacy of the
past, especially that of Romanticism. In his foreword to the
first American edition of *Demian* Thomas Mann wrote of its
author: "The best servitors of the new—Hesse is an example—
may be those who know and love the old and carry it over into
the new." In its form and technique *Demian* represents a bold
and revolutionary development abandoning the nineteenth-
century realist conventions and gradually merging into psychological probing of symbols, not merely for the sake of abstract knowledge or esthetic satisfaction but in order to examine
the basis of individual and social existence—the meaning of
life in our age. In this sense, it could be called one of the first
"existential" novels of the twentieth century.

When the novel first appeared and the identity of the author
was still not established, Thomas Mann wrote to the publisher
—who was also his own publisher—in the following enthusiastic
terms: "Please tell me: who is Emil Sinclair? How old is he?
Where does he live? His *Demian* has . . . made more impression
on me than anything else new for a long time. It is a fine, clever,
earnest and significant work! I read it . . . with the greatest emo-
tion and enjoyment." [14]

Mann goes on, however, to qualify his enthusiasm, pointing to the withdrawal from "life" (in the usual sense) into esthetic-spiritual abstraction: "One does not entirely escape a certain artistic contradiction in the story. It stands absolutely for life to the extent that the author's name is that of the narrator, and yet 'life'—in the sense for example of Tolystoy's 'Childhood and Boyhood'—is perhaps just its weak aspect, since it is in such high degree a composed piece of intellectual literary writing." Then Mann half withdraws this criticism: "But if one wishes, this contradiction is yet another attraction."

When *Demian* was first published in the U.S.A., it met with no response. In literature, realism, "life," provided the criteria for the novel. Today, thirty years later, it is not so easy to reject the work because of its esoteric, spiritual, abstract or "unreal" qualities.

The impact and the appeal of *Demian* are not limited to the two immediate postwar situations. A criticism of the old order may apply to any age in which individuals feel frustration and *Angst* and yet seek to realize themselves (*sich selbst verwirklichen*). Many today can share the feelings of Sinclair-Demian that the conventional mode of civilization leads to "affiliation and mass culture but nowhere to freedom and love", (III, 227) so that the community is only "a society held together by anxiety—inwardly decayed and decrepit and near collapse." Today people know exactly "how many grams of powder one requires to kill a man, but they do not know how to pray to God, they don't even know how to be content for an hour." As their world rushes toward the abyss of war, Sinclair concludes: "This world, as it is now, is intent on dying; it is bent on perishing and it will." Then, through the influence and proximity of Frau Eva (whose figure symbolizes death and birth in one), Sinclair has a visionary glimpse of a new possibility of life, of Goethe's paradoxical insight into "stirb und werde" (die and become). The war means both *Sterben* and *Werden,* and this is symbolized in the ending, which sees Demian dying and Sinclair changed and spiritually reborn. The ending points optimistically to the final stage in the triadic pattern of development—explicitly the Jungian triad superimposed upon the other triadic structures of religion and idealism.

CHAPTER 5

Three Novellen: Klingsor

THE THREE *Novellen* published in 1920 under this title have, at first glance, little in common beyond the initial "K" in the titles. The first story, "Kinderseele," portrays a crisis of conscience and guilt in a child of eleven. The second, "Klein und Wagner," seems to be the story of a criminal, his flight and suicide. The third, "Klingsors letzter Sommer," is concerned with the artist: the intensity of his experience of life and the problem of his creativity between magical insight and death wish.

All three share, of course, the strong autobiographical current that runs through Hesse's writing. But this alone would hardly connect the theme of childhood guilt and the creativity of the mature artist. These stories are, however, closely related to *Demian* in time and theme, and they, too, reflect a preoccupation with the war and the sense of crisis in art and in civilization.

"Kinderseele" ("A Child's Soul"), the tale of a young boy and a childish crisis over stolen figs, is by no means a child's story, and the first-person narrator is, in fact, looking back upon his boyhood experience with the adult's perceptive psychological awareness. The first-person narration, however, heightens the autobiographical background, as we visualize the austere bourgeois moral standards and rigorous pietistic faith of Hesse's parents living in what is plainly the small town of Calw. Marie Hesse's diary records on November 11, 1889: "Hermann's theft of figs discovered." [1]

It would be wrong, however, to see in the father figure a portrait of Johannes Hesse. The author has used his own family environment as the canvas on which he has painted a portrait which, despite family attributes, is more representative of Freud's concept of the father-son conflict: "I felt within me an inexplicable but overwhelming opposition to my father and toward everything that he expected and demanded of me" (III, 464).

In one sense, "Kinderseele" can be seen as a variation on the theme of *Demian*, giving another example of the individual's struggle toward maturity through incurring guilt and breaking away from the world of the father:

O God! O dear God! . . . I had stolen. I was no wounded hero returning from the battle. . . . I was a thief, I was a criminal. Up there no refuge awaited me, no bed and no sleep, no food and solace, no comfort and no forgetting. Guilt and criminal investigation were waiting for me.
It was then that I breathed . . . the cold ether of outer space, isolation, fate. (III, 453)

The hero's guilt and his rebellion against the actual father expand to embrace God and the cosmic order: "For I hate you, God, and I spit at your feet. You have tormented and flayed me, you have given commandments which no one can keep" (III, 445). Thus this apparently simple story of a childhood crisis in faith can be seen to symbolize, like the other two novellas, the crisis in European civilization brought to a head by the First World War. We catch glimpses of existential isolation, *Angst,* and meaninglessness:

Uneasiness and anxiety (*Angst*) weigh heavily on our hearts, and we seek and find the supposed causes outside ourselves, we see the world badly planned and directed, and everywhere we meet obstacles. . . . everything had combined into that feeling of impotence and despair that tells us . . . that this whole life is senseless and abhorrent. . . . I would always be an outsider, standing alone and uncertain, full of presentiments but without knowing. (III, 430–33)

The second story, "Klein und Wagner," is strikingly different, and the reader accustomed to the autobiographical element in Hesse may well wonder at this correct bourgeois banker who has lived for years a circumspect life with his wife and children and then suddenly absconds with a huge sum to Switzerland. The reader might imagine Klein's flight to lead to Italy, judging from the southern sights and sounds and the Italian names. It is, however, the Ticino—the Italian-speaking Swiss canton and its capital, Lugano, from which the Italian shore can be reached across the lake. Castiglione is actually a village on the Italian side of Lake Lugano but some distance up the eastern shoulder of Monte Generoso, while the town on the lakefront of the Italian enclave, Campione, is noted for its gambling casino (and its resistance to Italian tax collectors). While this seems the least autobiographical of the three stories, it is, in a deeper sense, the most personal, reflecting the collapse of Hesse's marriage and his "flight" from bourgeois, urban Berne to the southern Ticino and the crisis in the author's *Weltanschauung* of the *Demian* period and World War I.

A twin motif intertwines Richard Wagner (and especially *Lohengrin*) and a Swabian schoolmaster named Wagner who has murdered his wife and children and then committed suicide. Klein has suffered all his married life from an obsessional neurosis in which he is subconsciously drawn to commit the same bloody act while at the same time he is fascinated by Wagner's *Lohengrin:* the figure of the knight into whose past no one may inquire.

However, Klein is not merely a pathological figure but a symbolic one as well, and the story is more than a clinical exercise in psychoanalysis. One can, without doing violence to the tale, interpret Klein as a representative of European bourgeois society which is inwardly sick and disintegrating. Klein's (and Hesse's) suggested solution is "to let oneself go" (*sich fallen lassen*) into death or into the wholeness and oneness of the undifferentiated universe.

Heinz W. Puppe has demonstrated the close connection in this story between psychoanalysis and Eastern mysticism. He sees Klein passing through three stages of development:

In the first, which is prior to the narrated span embracing flight and death, Klein was a figure without a conscious will, driven this way and that by conventions. In the second stage he becomes conscious of himself, comprehends his dependence and tries to liberate himself. In the third he will leave himself entirely in the hands of his fate, a force beyond psychological and rational data.[3]

That so much of the story is taken up by the psychoanalytic theme symbolized by the two Wagners—namely the potential for good *and* for evil in the individual—is excused by Puppe on the ground that the Eastern mystical theme of the reality behind the veil of Maya lies in a realm beyond visualization and words. Not every reader will forgive Hesse so easily for hiding his major theme behind so much superficial preoccupation with psychology. And yet Puppe's analysis of the Eastern theme seems irrefutable, especially in the light of Hesse's later work, in particular *Siddhartha* and the *Lebenslauf*, "Dasa," in *Das Glasperlenspiel*.

Klein, in effect, enters into direct communication with the numinal world, and this simultaneously means extinction of the individual and his connection with Maya: "Letting oneself fall has also the positive meaning that Klein has submitted entirely to the 'guide in his own heart' and thereby to union with the all in one."[3]

This final act of suicide is described by Hesse, however, as "childishness, something that, to be sure, is not bad but comical and rather foolish" (III, 548). We are also told that "the fact that he let himself fall into the water and to his death would not have been necessary. He could just as well have let himself fall into life" (III, 549). The suicide is, therefore, of no importance, since it takes place in a world of temporality. The decisive fact is that Klein, in his last moments, "lets himself go." The suicide is no longer flight.[4]

Puppe admits that this inner meaning may seem implausible to many readers, especially since the suicide act immediately follows a murderous impulse, as Klein leans over the sleeping figure of the woman: "Now it came upon him. Now he, Wagner, was standing beside the bed of a sleeping woman and was searching for the knife!—No, he wouldn't. No, he was not crazy!"

To the extent that Hesse intended the major theme to be this Eastern mystical solution to the problem of existential anxiety it seems that the *Novelle* must be judged as a limited success, even though the cause of partial failure is inherent in the fact that the ineffable defies concrete expression. But the psychological theme is of great interest, especially when the figures are seen as symbolic representations of certain aspects of Western man. The connection with *Demian* and with the essays on Dostoyevsky is plain when Klein says to the dancer, Teresina: "You don't wish to be other than what you are, no matter whether good or evil. Isn't that the very thing you saw in me?" (III, 510). We are reminded again of Emil Sinclair when we read: "Wrestling and despairing, Klein struggled with his *Dämon.*" And the Abraxas-theme—the Dostoyevskian paradox of good and evil—rings out in Klein's reflection: "He was aware that everything painful, everything stupid, everything evil was transformed into its opposite if one succeeded in recognizing it as God, if one pursued it to its deepest roots, which extended far beyond weal and woe, good and evil" (III, 525–26).

The way in which the philosophical and the psychological themes were fused in Hesse's mind is clearly shown in a diary entry from the year 1920:

Nirvana, as I understand it, is the liberating step behind the *principium individuationis*, hence in religious terms the return of the individual soul to the universal spirit (*Allseele*). It is another question, whether one is to desire, strive for and hasten this return or not. If God sends me out into the world and causes me to exist as an individual, is it then my task to come back to the universal oneness as quickly and easily as possible—or am I not, on the other hand, to fulfill God's will just by letting myself go (in a story I called it "sich fallen lassen"), that I atone with him for his desire to split himself and extend his life over and over again in individual beings?[5]

"Klein and Wagner" is thematically close to *Demian* but lacks the impact and the deeper suggestiveness of the latter because it can too readily be conceived as a criminal story laced with somewhat pathological psychoanalysis and ending in a suicide the metaphysical import of which is apt to escape the reader.

The third story, "Klingsors letzter Sommer," which provides the title for the triptych, differs in many ways from the other two. For one thing, it is subjective, personal, and autobiographical in a new way, anticipating *Die Morgenlandfahrt;* for it is a work which can be read with a key: a playful game with real persons and places. Many of the names are only thinly disguised, as Laguno for Lugano, Kareno for Carona. Others are more esoteric: Louis the Cruel for Hesse's friend the Swiss painter Louis Moilliet (in my view a playful ironic antonym of the association evoked by *mouillé*—soft, wet—and not an allusion to Nietzsche as suggested by Ernst Rose[6]). In this category falls the identification of Klingsor as Hesse, for Klingsor is the name of a powerful magician in Wolfram von Eschenbach's *Parzival* and occurs in Novalis' unfinished novel *Heinrich von Ofterdingen;* and one needs to know Hesse's occasional playful references to himself as "the magician" and his more consistent use of "magic" for "art" and "magician" for "artist" as in the Magic Theater of *Der Steppenwolf.* Ruth Wenger, who four years later was to become Hesse's second wife, is portrayed as the queen of the mountains from the parrot house in Kareno.

This is an intriguing game for connoisseurs and insiders, but the major appeal and importance of the work is not to be sought on this level. While it treats again, from another point of view, the self-abandonment or self-release of the individual, there are two major differences: this time the protagonist is an artist, and his self-release therefore involves expressing or creating what is within and expending himself in the process. Secondly, the work is linked with the Expressionist movement not only in theme but also in spirit, form, and language.

From painting came the initial impetus and the name "Expressionism." In this movement there was an unusual amount of cross-fertilization between literature, the plastic arts, and painting.[7] Among the artists whose work influenced Expressionism one may mention Georges Braque, Barlach, Franz Marc, Kirchner, Kandinsky, Kokoschka, Paul Klee, and Van Gogh.[8] Some attained prominence in more than one field, e.g. Barlach in engraving, sculpture, and literature, Kokoschka and Kandinsky in painting and literature.

In the present story, too, the autobiographical element is strong, as Hesse at this time plunged into painting of a pronounced Expressionist tendency. As in *Unterm Rad* and other works, Hesse projects himself mainly in two figures: the painter Klingsor and the latter's friend, the poet Hermann, who is also called Thu Fu. But, as Boulby has observed, there are elements of self-portraiture also in Li Tai Pe, in the Armenian astrologer and even in Louis the Cruel. "There is fragmentation of the ego. The powerful dialogue between the astrologer and Klingsor-Li Tai Pe is that between ... acceptance and frenzy, the seer and the artist." [9]

Martini sees Expressionism characterized by "the will of the individual to metamorphosis, however diverse the process, whether in the form of nihilistic extinction or infinite exaltation, or mystical oblation, in religious, ethical, political, social or a creative-vitalistic sense. ..." Klingsor exemplifies the "creative-vitalistic sense" as the artist feels in the lush, hot July in the Ticino the creative and procreative urge. The language of this work can be described in the words which Martini uses of Expressionist writers in general: "The new language of the inner soul, of the ecstatic dream-world and of an unrestrained subjectivism." [10]

The ecstatic-vitalistic element dominates the figure of Klingsor who has "burned the candle at both ends ... now with a jubilant, now with a sobbing feeling of expending himself in a mad whirl, of combustion, with a desperate eagerness to empty the beaker completely, and with a deep-seated, secret anxiety before the end" (III, 558).

Martini speaks of the Expressionists' intensity of feeling which expands to embrace the world and even the cosmos: "for the goals of the new expressionistic gestures are intensity between torment and ecstasy, even to the frenzy of scream or stammer, pathos of vision unto the infinite and truthfulness to denudation." [11] Thus Klingsor's consciousness expands:

Hoch sassen sie in schwebender Schaukel überm Abgrund der Welt und Nacht, Vögel in goldenem Käfig, ohne Heimat, ohne Schwere, den Sternen gegenüber. Sie sangen, die Vögel, sangen exotische Lieder, sie phantasierten aus berauschten Herzen in die Nacht, in den Himmel, in den Wald, in das fragwürdige, bezauberte Weltall hinein. Antwort kam von Stern und Mond, von Baum und Gebirg, Goethe sass da und Hafis, heiss duftete Aegypten und innig Griechenland herauf, Mozart lächelte, Hugo Wolf spielte den Flügel in der irren Nacht. ...

Klingsor, König der Nacht, hohe Krone im Haar, rückgelehnt auf steinernem Sitz, dirigierte den Tanz der Welt, gab den Takt an, rief den Mond hervor, liess die Eisenbahn verschwinden. (III, 582–83) [12]

Three Novellen

Martini declares that Hesse, in "Klingsors letzter Sommer," wrote the inner biography of the Expressionist artist. But despite these thematic and formal contacts with Expressionism, this work stands only on the periphery of this literary movement. In June, 1918, Hesse published in *Die Neue Rundschau* an answer to Kasimir Edschmid's essay on "Expressionismus in der Dichtung." Hesse adopted a reserved attitude to the categorical Expressionist doctrines and turned upon Edschmid a phrase which the latter had used to pillory Impressionism: "But with all the good will in the world I just cannot find that the cosmic feeling among Expressionists [one may think of Mombert or J. R. Becher] is expressed in any way other than in ecstatic babbling." While rejecting the extreme demands of Expressionists to throw out the old—"whoever up to now has loved Keller or Fontane, Storm or Ibsen, is not going to throw them away"—Hesse makes a statement of his personal stand which shows a considerable sympathy with some Expressionist elements:

> For as far as I am concerned, in my most private theology and mythology I call Expressionism the resounding of the cosmic, the reminder of the primordial homeland of the human race, the timeless sense of time, the lyrical talking of the individual with the world, confession and avowal of self, the experience of self in random images or metaphors.[18]

These words of Hesse could be taken as a programmatic statement for "Klingsors letzter Sommer." Even the apparently disjointed, fragmented character of the narrative, which reminds one of so much Expressionist writing, carries the underlying theme of the individual—in this case the visual artist—expressing and avowing what is within him, accepting and living his fate, as in *Demian* and the two preceding stories.

In *Klingsor* one finds allusions to the bird image and the Frau Eva figure of *Demian*, to the death of Klein in the boat, and to the sense of crisis experienced by the Europeans:

> The tired, greedy, savage, childlike and over-civilized man of our late epoch, the dying European welcoming death: sensitized by every longing, sick from every vice, enthusiastically inspired by the knowledge of his decline, ready for every progress, ripe for every regression, all exhilaration and at the same time all exhaustion, resigned to

fate and pain as the morphine addict to his poison, isolated, emptied, ancient, at the same time Faust and Karamazov. . . . (III, 610)

Despite occasional extravagances which an age no longer attuned to Expressionism might call turgid, "Klingsors letzter Sommer" is one of Hesse's most significant works of shorter prose fiction. Its strength and merit derive in part from the convergence of the author's inmost spiritual situation with the spirit of the age: the turbulent, rebellious, disillusioned war and postwar generation which alternated between ecstatic feelings of new birth and premonitions of doom. Hesse felt his personal and metaphysical worlds shattered by the war, the divorce and the separation from his children and from all his familiar milieux. It seemed an end. But then the translation to the Ticino, the feeling of new freedom there, the color and the lush subtropical environment and his new interest in painting: all these heralded not an end but something like a new birth. This is soberly indicated in the closing lines of *Klingsor* which, almost with the effect of Romantic *Stimmungsbrechung* (deliberate shattering of the created illusion), point not to death but to Klingsor's new life in matter-of-fact terms: "After these whiplashed days he placed the finished picture in the empty unused kitchen and locked the door. He never exhibited it. Then he took veronal and slept through a day and a night. Then he washed, shaved, put on fresh clothing, drove into town and bought fruit and cigarettes as a present for Gina."

CHAPTER 6

Siddhartha: *The Way Within*

I Vita activa

THE first part of *Siddhartha* was written in the winter of
1919, at the end of that first exuberant productive year in
Montagnola. Hesse has told us how the composition was borne
along on a surge of creative energy which suddenly came to an
end, and he was not able to complete the work until two years
later:

Nearly two years ago [i.e. 1919] was my last high point . . . the
fullest, most exuberant, most industrious and most glowing [year]
of my life. . . . And now for almost a year and a half I have been
living like a snail, slowly and thriftily. . . . I have produced nothing
but the first part of *Siddhartha* and the beginning of the second
which has bogged down. Instead I have painted and read and inwardly moved closer to the India of gods and idolatry. . . .[1]

One of the difficulties was no doubt the finding of a suitable
conclusion, since it involved conveyance in the logic of language
of something essentially beyond words, i.e., magical insight.
In a later edition, *Siddhartha* appeared with other stories
under the title *Der Weg nach Innen* (*The Way Within*),[2] and

it is in fact Hesse's most introspective work, apparently glorifying the *vita passiva*. But Hesse's writing is characterized by pulsation between active and passive poles, and this particular polarity was to become a major theme in *Das Glasperlenspiel*. It is well, then, to recall that in the very years when this work of pronounced Eastern meditation and introspection was taking shape, its author was engaged in very active battles on several other fronts. With the end of the war, while physically withdrawing to an isolated mode of existence, Hesse entered the lists to work for the establishment of a healthy, peaceful outlook in which the new German democracy could flourish.

Zarathustras Wiederkehr (*Zarathustra's Return*, 1920) was a clarion call to the Germans—especially to the German youth—to shake off not only despair and recrimination but also the "false gods" of commercialism, nationalism, and militarism which had led the nation into the abyss of defeat. In a commentary on this work Hesse pointed out that the misunderstood and misused Nietzsche seemed "the last solitary representative of the German spirit . . . who had finally become anti-German in revulsion against the cultural crudity of the Wilhelmian era." [3]

In the last years of the war and in the first months after its end, Hesse's essays are permeated with a new biting satire. *Der Europäer* (*The European*) of January, 1918, envisages the Europeans fighting on indefinitely with ever more refined methods of destruction, until God finds it necessary to send another flood in order to end the carnage. But as the flood mounts, the embattled European nations build higher and higher platforms from which to bombard each other:

Ensconced in towers, human heroism preserved itself with touching faithfulness to the very end. While Europe and all the world was being inundated and deluged, from the last towering steel turrets searchlights kept on glittering through the moist grayness of the perishing earth and projectiles still soared to and fro in elegant arcs from the cannons. Thus the shooting was carried on heroically to the last hour. (VII, 105)

Finally, there is only one surviving European floundering in a lifejacket. After he is picked up by the patriarch and taken on board the ark, the inhabitants entertain him with their special skills. The European has nothing to offer but his vaunted Western intellect, of which he can present no evidence, and so they accept him as the joker; but many doubt his capacity to make any positive contribution to the new world. The patriarch intervenes to point out that God has looked after this, for as the sole survivor of his species he cannot reproduce himself like all the others. The next day, the tip of the sacred mountain appears above the receding flood waters, heralding the new beginning on earth.

Wenn der Krieg noch zwei Jahre dauert (end of 1917) and its sequel *Wenn der Krieg noch fünf Jahre dauert* (*If the War Lasts Five More Years*, 1918) project an ironic vision of a dehumanized world. A modern Rip van Winkle is discovered by the authorities. Although he brilliantly passes all medical and intelligence tests, he is lodged in an asylum because he knows nothing of the war and the strange restrictions it has imposed on life.

The months after the armistice saw the appearance of Hesse's essays "Das Reich," "Der Weg der Liebe" ("The Way of Love"), and "Brief an einen jungen Deutschen" ("Letter to a Young German"). Early in 1919 appeared the first number of *Vivos voco*, a new periodical founded and edited by Hesse and Richard Woltereck. The message of the title is plain: to summon the living to build a better world. For three years, Hesse himself wrote a large number of articles and reviews. In 1922 he retired as editor but continued to contribute until 1924. His work in this journal drew a considerable number of threatening and vituperative letters, from reactionary nationalistic elements, which Hesse used with devastating effect to pillory the standpoint of the correspondents in "Hassbriefe" (II, [1921-22], 235–39).

In this period falls the separate publication of *Blick ins Chaos* (*Glimpse into Chaos*, 1920), containing the two major Dostoyevsky essays. Hesse saw in Dostoyevsky and his characters (and in Nietzsche) an intuitive anticipation of the descent into anarchy and an ensuing new morality, prefiguring the fate of Western Europe. *Blick ins Chaos* was instrumental in extending Hesse's fame beyond the German-speaking world. It was translated into English and reprinted, in whole or in part, in several journals. Among those impressed was T. S. Eliot, who visited Hesse and enlisted him as collaborator on his new periodical *Criterion*. As it turned out, only one article by Hesse appeared, entitled "New German Poetry." Mr. Eliot upon being asked about his meeting with Hesse and why there had been no further contributions, replied in a letter of September 16, 1960:

My attention was first drawn to Hermann Hesse by my friend Sydney Schiff, who was also known as a novelist under the name Stephen Hudson [translator of *Blick ins Chaos*]. He gave me *Blick ins Chaos* to read and I was very much impressed by it. A little later— I think in 1921 or 22—I was staying for a short time in Lugano and took an opportunity of going up to visit Hermann Hesse in his mountain retreat. We had, as I remember, a very interesting conversation. He must have done most of the talking himself as my ability to understand German when spoken exceeds my ability to speak it. . . . I do not know why there was only one contribution by him, or whether I solicited further work, for I do remember that I was much impressed by the man and would, I suppose, have been very glad to have further contributions from him.[4]

In spite of his vigorous polemics on behalf of the delicate infant Weimar republic, Hesse became increasingly pessimistic about the future of democracy in Germany. In 1923 he formally dissociated himself from his fatherland by becoming a naturalized Swiss.

By 1922–23 Hesse was engaged on another front—the battle for existence. He depended on royalties from publication in Germany, and the ultimate effect of the inflationary spiral was to cut off his income entirely, since in the final weeks of the monetary crisis sums despatched from Germany became entirely worthless by the time they were received in Switzerland. For a while Hesse was helped by local friends, and he eked out a modest living by selling for 285 Swiss francs holograph copies of his fairy tale *Piktors Verwandlungen* (*Piktor's Metamorphoses*), illustrated with his Expressionistic water-color paintings (different in each copy). This tale emphasizes the motif of change and the yearning for wholeness. Having been transformed into a tree at his wish, Piktor pines away, for "one can see it every day in all creatures: If they do not possess the gift of metamorphosis, they decay in time with melancholy and atrophy, and their beauty is lost." A beautiful girl redeems Piktor by becoming one with the tree and restoring it to wholeness and the possibility of infinite transformations. "Piktor was no longer a bent old tree, now he sang jubilantly Piktoria, Viktoria. He was transformed. And because this time he had attained the right eternal transformation, because he had become a whole from a half, from this hour he could transform himself as much as he wished." [5]

This light-hearted tale reminds us, therefore, both, of the financial plight of the author in the early twenties and of the themes which were uppermost in his mind at the time, for Siddhartha's quest, too, is for wholeness, oneness, and involves constant transformation.

II   *Siddhartha's Quest*

The opening chapter of *Siddhartha* presents a pair of friends, both sons of Brahmans; but Govinda is the devoted follower while Siddhartha is marked as leader. Siddhartha overcomes his father in a gentle but inflexible contest of wills reflecting Indian passive resistance. Behind this Indian mask it is easy to glimpse Hesse's self-assertion vis-à-vis his own father and the priestly path ordained for him.

Both friends abandon home, family, and caste to join the Samanas, thus becoming indigent "holy men." For the images of life are "not worth a glance, everything deceived, everything stank, stank of falseness, everything gave an illusion of meaning and happiness and beauty, and yet everything was unacknowledged decomposition" (III, 626). At this stage, the aim is an ascetic denial of life, a suppression of the ego:

One goal stood before Siddhartha: to become empty, empty of thirst, of wish, empty of dream, of pain and pleasure. To die away from himself, to be no longer I, to find peace in his emptied heart, in his de-individualized thinking to be receptive to miracles, that was his goal. If the ego was completely overcome and extinguished, if every yearning and every instinct died in his heart, then the ultimate had to awaken, the inmost essence which is no longer ego, the great secret. (III, 626)

After three years, the friends have steeled the flesh against the assaults of the senses and of the external world. But Siddhartha, finding no further progress and no ultimate goal attainable on this path, goes with Govinda in search of Gautama the Buddha, of whom each finger "spoke, breathed, exuded, gleamed truth"

(III, 638). But it is the living presence not the preaching which convinces. Therefore Siddhartha goes on his way, rejecting the temptation to linger among the Buddha's disciples who receive Govinda. Wandering now on his solitary way, he asks himself:

"What is it that you have been trying to learn from teachers and doctrines, and which they who taught you much nevertheless could not teach?" And he found: "It was the ego whose meaning and nature I wanted to fathom. It was the ego from which I wanted to free myself, which I wanted to overcome. But I could not overcome it, I could only deceive it. I could not flee from it, only hide from it. . . . I was fleeing from myself! I was seeking Atman [Sanskrit *atman*: breath, self, supreme spirit, universal self], I was seeking Brahma [a personification of the ultimate absolute or cosmic principle], . . . But in the process I was losing myself. . . .
I shall become acquainted with this ego, the secret of Siddhartha." (III, 645–46)

Now we see the polarity motif in operation, as Siddhartha from the ascetic pole of deadened sense perceptions awakes to the physical world: "He had to begin his life anew completely from the beginning" (III, 648).

Early in the second part, Siddhartha's quest embraces the oneness that transcends all polarities:

No, this world of learning belonged to the phenomenal world and it led to no goal if one killed off the fortuitous ego of the senses only to fatten the fortuitous ego of thoughts and theories. Both were nice things, thoughts as well as instincts, but the ultimate lay beyond both; it was necessary to listen to both, to play with both, neither to despise nor overvalue both, but from both to harken to the secret voices of the inmost being. (III, 652)

Siddhartha reaches the river, which is an obvious symbol of the boundary between two worlds and two ways of life. This river symbol soon assumes syncretic power, becoming also the major symbol of oneness, as its voice whispers the mystic syllable "om."

Beyond the river, Siddhartha comes to the city and wins the courtesan Kamala who initiates him into sexual love, while he gains wealth and power in the merchants' world. His strength in love and business had been derived, however, from his years of

physical and spiritual training. In the course of time, his
stamina and concentration weaken. This reciprocal dependence
of "nature" and "spirit" offers one of many points of comparison with Thomas Mann's treatment of the theme in *The Transposed Heads*. The major difference lies in Mann's hilariously
ironical and satirical handling of the material, while Hesse
maintains an exalted poetic tone.

Almost the opposite process takes place in *Das Glasperlenspiel*
when Joseph Knecht finds the one-sided "spiritual" Castalian
atmosphere too rarefied. In fact, Knecht's diagnosis of impending crisis stresses the necessity of embracing the polar elements
of intellectuality and sensuality. Basically, the situation is similar in both works, and both protagonists in their actions stress
metamorphosis.

In the last night spent with Kamala, Siddhartha realizes "how
closely sensual lust is related to death" (III, 677). Death is
metamorphosis, as Rilke reminds us in the *Sonnets to Orpheus*
and especially in "Wolle die Wandlung. O sei für die Flamme
begeistert" ("Will to be transformed. O show zeal for the
flame"). We are prepared, then, for the next step on Siddhartha's Way as, on the next day, he leaves Kamala, his wealthy
merchant patron Kamaswami, and abandons the life of the
Kindermenschen (child-people).⁸

He wanders back through the forest to the river, which is now
no longer the boundary but Rilke's central "turning point." In
the polar oscillation of Siddhartha's life, he comes to rest on the
river. But his return first brings him to the verge of committing
suicide. "He was filled with satiety, full of misery, full of
death. There was nothing left in the world to entice him, give
him pleasure or comfort . . . there was no aim left . . . but to
make an end of this miserable and disgraceful life" (III, 681–
82). He "lets himself fall" into the river "towards death" (thus
reintroducing the motif of "Klein und Wagner"). But from
the depths of his soul "the holy 'om'" resounds and he perceives
the folly of his action.

He sinks into restorative sleep and on awaking finds Govinda
watching over him—a temporary reversal of their roles. Siddhartha tries to explain his quest. "It is the same with me as with
you. I am traveling nowhere. I am only wandering—a pilgrim.
. . . I have had to sin, in order to be able to live again" (III,
686–90).

He resolves to remain by this river of life and time and becomes the helper of the old ferryman Vasudeva. This figure evokes multiple associations. Apart from the Eastern attributes, which we shall examine in the next section, one is reminded of Charon and his duty to ferry the souls of the deceased across the river Styx. He represents essentially the *vita passiva,* but not entirely so, since he exercises a helpful function for his fellow humans. He has gained magical insight into the oneness and simultaneity of life, so that all life flows to him.

Siddhartha, however, faces one more trial when Kamala arrives to die in his arms, leaving the son born after Siddhartha's disappearance. He strives to win the boy's affection and to keep him, but the son rebels against the father, repeating more violently Siddhartha's gentler self-liberation from the paternal world effected a generation before. Gradually Siddhartha begins to understand "that with his son not peace and happiness had come to him, but suffering and worry" (III, 706). He becomes again a "child-person," losing his equanimity and serenity. After the boy's escape and the vain pursuit, Siddhartha, consoled by Vasudeva, gradually absorbs the lesson of the river:

> All voices, all aims, all yearning, all suffering, all pleasure, all good and all evil, all together made up the world. Everything together was the river of events, was the music of life. And if Siddhartha harkened . . . to the river . . . he heard all, the whole, the oneness and then the great song of the thousand voices consisted of a single word, om: perfection. . . . In this hour Siddhartha ceased to fight his fate, ceased to suffer. (III, 720–21)

After Vasudeva's death, Siddhartha inherits the office of ferryman and absorbs the inner awareness symbolized both by his predecessor and by the river. The last chapter brings back Govinda who sees that Siddhartha has "found the Way." But the efforts of Siddhartha to express this way in words are doomed to failure, since the "Way Within" for one individual defies formulation for another. "Knowledge can be imparted but not wisdom" (III, 742). As Demian has taught us, each individual has to become *himself.* However, Siddhartha's efforts to communicate with Govinda provide many interesting glimpses. He asserts, for example: "Time is not real, Govinda. . . . And if time is not real, then the span which seems to lie between world and eternity, between torment and bliss, between good and evil is also an illusion" (III, 725). And again: "Love seems, Govinda, to be the main thing" (III, 729).

While the teaching of Siddhartha cannot convince Govinda, the presence and countenance of Siddhartha remind him of the sensation he felt in the presence of Gautama Buddha, and Govinda realizes that "this is a saint" (III, 730). The pedagogical importance of the living example later becomes a major motif in the ending of Joseph Knecht's life in *Das Glasperlenspiel*.

III   *East and West*

Despite its brevity, *Siddhartha* may properly be called a *Bildungsroman,* sharing many features of this genre examined in *Demian.* But Hesse published it under the rubric "Eine indische Dichtung" ("An Indian Poetic Work"). When I visited him in Montagnola in 1957, he showed me several of the translations into Indian languages and spoke with interest of the work's recent success in the subcontinent. But in fact it is an interesting compound of Eastern and Western ingredients.

We have previously discussed the Eastern influences on Hesse and his affinity for elements of Eastern thought. In *Siddhartha,* the Indian milieu is the more effective for its temporal distance. When we get back to legendary times, we lose the sense of differentiation and come nearer the oneness of the human race. On the other hand, the legendary epoch of Gautama the Buddha provides a more remote background for Hesse's portrayal of himself or his Eastern alter ego.

The name Siddhartha has a double function, since it is a link with Buddha, who bore the name in his secular life, and at the same time signifies "the one who has found the Way." Vasudeva is one of the names of Krishna and suggests the meaning "he in whom all things abide and who abides in all." [7] Kamala may be associated with Kama, the Hindu god of love and desire. Kamaswami combines *kama* and *swami,* suggesting "master of the sensuous and material pleasures of life."

Hesse's *Siddhartha* is not intended to portray the life of Gautama the Buddha but he used the name and many other attributes to reflect the legendary atmosphere and prefigure the pattern of his hero's transformations. Both Siddhartha and Buddha were unusual children. Buddha left his wife and son to become an ascetic, as Siddhartha leaves his beloved Kamala and his unborn son to take up the ascetic, contemplative life. Both spent time among mendicant ascetics studying yoga. Buddha spent several years meditating by a river and Siddhartha's last years are spent in ferryman's service on the river. Buddha's revelations came to him under the Bo-tree while Siddhartha arrives at his final decision under the mango tree. Under the tree Buddha had a visionary experience of all his previous existences and the interconnection of all things, and Siddhartha's final magic vision also embraces simultaneity and oneness.

With all these Eastern allusions, attitudes, and legendary motifs, the reader may be lulled into accepting the work as basically Indian. However, Rudolf Pannwitz has pointed out the polar tension between East and West which underlies it:

Siddhartha is an Indian . . . contemporary of Buddha. He follows the ancient Indian ways but stops at each station and complements it by an opposing one, so that he reveals himself as a European . . . determined by the rhythm of Heraclitus. . . . [His European origin is further revealed] by the fact that he does not tarry in any lawful order and preordained role. Therefore for him there is no solution nor release that can satisfy him and free him from the demands of the subjective ego.[8]

Siddhartha recognizes the preeminence of Buddha's teaching and that he [Buddha] has found the Way. But Siddhartha cannot follow him for two reasons: first, because the European element in him prevents him from entering into anything fixed and prescribed; second, because Buddha is the redeemer not in a positive way by fulfilling, but negatively by overcoming and annihilating the world.

There is, therefore, an underlying Western Faustian quality in Siddhartha, which becomes almost explicit when Siddhartha exclaims "Immer habe ich nach Erkenntnis gedürstet" (III, 630: "I have always thirsted for cognition"), echoing Faust in his opening monologue "Dass ich erkenne was die Welt/Im Innersten zusammenhält" ("That I may have cognition of what holds the world together in its inmost essence"). Siddhartha exclaims "I have devoted much time . . . O Govinda in order to learn this: that one can learn nothing," recalling Faust's complaint "Und sehe, dass wir nichts wissen können/Das will mir schier das Herz verbrennen" ("And I perceive that we are not capable of attaining knowledge. This almost burns up my heart").

If Siddhartha, therefore, has Western activist well-springs deep within him, Govinda represents passive Oriental acceptance. The two friends thus present polar contrasts which together make a whole, thereby in a sense prefiguring the theme of the quest for oneness. Basically, their positions amount to Western affirmation and Eastern negation of life. Siddhartha's final stand, however, is not clear—reminding us of the author's difficulty in bringing the novel to a conclusion.

In his last stage, Siddhartha peers with what we may call "magical insight" behind the veil of Maya to realize the illusion of individuation and to glimpse the essential oneness and simultaneity of all things, as symbolized in the river and its whispered syllable "om." This is obviously Eastern, but in his attempt to convey his inner vision to Govinda, Siddhartha reveals two pronounced Western and Christian components: activity, experience, striving (in the Faustian tradition) and love or *caritas* (Franciscan in its universality). In addition, there is the element of divine grace, which has a Protestant ring; and the concept of metamorphosis seems at times closer to Western development and progress than to the Oriental eternal return through metempsychosis. All four elements can be glimpsed in the following excerpt:

> All sin bears grace within it. . . . I have experienced in my body and soul that I was badly in need of sin. I needed lust, striving for worldly goods and vanity, and I needed the most humiliating despair . . . in order to learn to love the world . . . to love it and rejoice in being part of it. . . . I can love a stone, Govinda, and also a tree or a piece of bark. Those are things, and one can love things. But words I cannot love. . . . Love, above all, O Govinda, seems to me the chief thing. To see through the world, to explain it, to despise it may be the concern of great thinkers. But I am only concerned with being able to love the world; not to despise it and hate it and myself but to be able to regard all creatures with love and admiration and reverence. (III, 726–29)

Even the paradoxical term "child-people" discloses its full significance near the end when Siddhartha has vainly pursued his son right back to the grave of Kamala:

Although he was nearing fulfillment and was enduring his last wound, it seemed to him nevertheless that these child-people were his brothers; their vanities, lusts, and silliness lost their ridiculousness for him and became understandable, became even worthy of reverence for him. (III, 715)

The doctrine of love and the stress on individual experience in finding the Way suggest a Protestant element; for as Hesse observed in 1931: "The fact that my *Siddhartha* stresses not cognition but love, that it rejects dogma and makes experience of oneness the central point, may be felt as a tendency to return to Christianity, even to a truly Protestant faith" (VII, 372).

The figure of Buddha is recalled as Siddhartha says of him "his deeds and his life are more dear to me than his preaching, the gestures of his hand more important than his opinions. Not in talking, not in thinking do I see his greatness but only in doing and living" (III, 729).

This anti-intellectual tendency can hardly be categorized as Western or Eastern. It may be related, however, to the skepticism vis-à-vis Western rational and technological civilization arising out of the growing disillusionment in the postwar years. This antipathy to a technological society will reappear in *Steppenwolf*, but ultimately, in *Das Glasperlenspiel*, it will be modified in a searching analysis of what is really enduring in civilization.

IV *Style and Structure*

The mood evoked by *Siddhartha* is that of serenity, of a poetic, exalted world on a higher plane. While serenity is dominant, an opposite undercurrent of dramatic tension reminds us of the similarly subtle effects of Adalbert Stifter's smoothly stylized poetic prose. There we encounter a similar shift from a serene outer world to the problematic inner world. This inner realm is the scene of repeated crises. The initial rebellion against the father is followed by Siddhartha's renunciation of the world to join the Samanas; they, in turn, are abandoned in order to hear Buddha. The rejection of Buddha's teaching and the consequent parting from Govinda are followed by the rejection of asceticism in favor of the sensual and material life. This, too, is abandoned, and the return to the river leads to the brink of suicide, which is followed by Kamala's arrival and death.

Only after the tense battle to win his son does Siddhartha penetrate into the serene sense of cosmic unity.

In the most dramatic moments, the sedate style is slightly modified, as when Siddhartha reaches the decision to end it all:

> With a distorted face he stared into the water, saw his face mirrored and spat at it. In deep fatigue he loosened one arm from the tree trunk and turned a little, in order to let himself fall vertically, in order to succumb finally. With eyes shut he plunged down to death.
>
> Then a sound quivered from remote layers of his soul, from past epochs of his tired life. It was a word, a syllable, which he spoke without thinking, with a lilting voice, to himself, the old opening and closing word of all Brahman prayers. . . . When the sound "om" touched Siddhartha's ear, his benumbed mind suddenly awoke and realized the folly of his action. (III, 683)

But the divergences in style here are minimal—a slightly more concise, clipped expression with stress on the verbs of action— while the features which mark the style of the whole are still present, namely a triadic pattern of sentence and paragraph structure, intensive repetition and the beginning of sentences with adverb or predicate, thus producing a chant-like rhythm: "Schön war die Welt, bunt war die Welt, seltsam und rätselhaft war die Welt!" [9]

The following paragraph offers a striking illustration of these stylistic features:

> Langsam blüte, langsam reifte in Siddhartha die Erkenntnis, das Wissen darum, was eigentlich Weisheit sei, was seines langen Suchens Ziel sei. Es war nichts als eine Bereitschaft der Seele, eine Fähigkeit, eine geheime Kunst, jeden Augenblick, mitten im Leben, den Gedanken der Einheit denken, die Einheit fühlen und einatmen zu können. Langsam blühte dies in ihm auf, strahlte ihm aus Vasudevas altem Kindergesicht wider: Harmonie, Wissen um die ewige Vollkommenheit der Welt, Lächeln, Einheit. [10]

The passage opens with an adverb and is constructed on a triadic pattern of three sentences: opening statement, development, and conclusion. This arrangement is especially appropriate here in summing up Siddhartha's quest and his attainment of magical insight. The repetition reinforces the three-beat rhythm.

Ziolkowski has pointed out the ubiquity of the beatific smile as the symbol of fulfillment in the novels from *Siddhartha* to *Das Glasperlenspiel*.[11] At the moment preceding Vasudeva's death, this smile is transferred to Siddhartha in a mystical sharing. The style of this passage strikingly reflects the features we have discussed and which are more directly apparent in the original German text:

Hell glänzte Vasudevas Lächeln, über all den Runzeln seines alten Antlitzes schwebte es leuchtend, wie über all den Stimmen des Flusses das Om schwebte. Hell glänzte sein Lächeln, als er den Freund anblickte. und hell glänzte nun auch auf Siddharthas Gesicht dasselbe Lächeln auf. Seine Wunde blühte, sein Leid strahlte, sein Ich war in die Einheit geflossen.[12]

Imbedded in the last sentence, however, is a double oxymoron: "His wound flourished, his pain shone radiantly." This reminder of the theme of polarity is striking here at the moment when it is transcended by and embraced in a higher magical unity.

The inner structure of the novel is based not on the outer division into two parts; but, as Ziolkowski observes:

the book falls into three natural sections: Siddhartha's life at home, among the Samanas, and with Buddha (four chapters); his life with Kamala and among the "child-people" of the city (four chapters); and his life with Vasudeva on the river (four chapters). . . . Temporally and spatially the periods are delimited by Siddhartha's initial crossing of the river and by his subsequent return to it. . . . And the river, as the natural symbol of synthesis, is the natural border between the realms of spirit and sense in which Siddhartha attempts to live before he achieves the synthesis upon its very banks. What we have, in other words, is a projection of Siddhartha's inner development into the realm of space: the landscape of the soul.[13]

This is a perceptive analysis of the structure, which shows awareness of the dual symbolic function of the river as both a boundary dividing separate stages on the Way and as the unitary principle itself.

Repetition, which permeates the style in the form of recurring words, phrases, and sentences, leads structurally to the use of leitmotifs, many of which we have mentioned, such as the river symbol and the beatific smile. Among others, one may mention the bird (carried over from *Demian*), which occurs in a dream and exists as Kamala's pet. It becomes symbolic, however, in the phrase "Dead was the bird in his heart" (III, 681).

In addition to leitmotifs, parallelisms also reinforce the unity of the work. Siddhartha's initial break with his father is paralleled by the situation between himself and his son. Buddha smiles and preaches the Way to Govinda and Siddhartha. At the end, it is Siddhartha who attempts to preach or explain his Way to Govinda. Again it is not the words but the smile, the face, and the hands which convince.

Such a style has obviously little to do with realism. Hesse deprecated the tendency in our age to attribute excessive importance to "so-called reality" in the shape of physical events and things, especially of a technological nature.[14] Freedman has used the term "lyrical novel" for works such as this, and of all of Hesse's works *Siddhartha* fits this description best.[15] Siddhartha's quest transcends "reality," and the narrative manner is intended to carry the reader into an elevated, poetic, legendary, or "magical" world. In fact, in unity of style, structure, and meaning *Siddhartha* represents Hesse's highest achievement.

In spite of the Western ingredients, it must be admitted that Siddhartha's third and final stage stresses Eastern passivity and introspection. But this was Siddhartha's Way, not Govinda's nor anyone else's. It was not Hesse's Way either, or at least not his final station; and the most characteristic leitmotif in the work is that of "Erwachen" (awakening) to a new beginning.

Hesse's next major work, *Der Steppenwolf,* offers a complete contrast, replacing serenity by stridency, placing the individual problem in a social context and stressing the contrast between the "inner" and "outer" worlds for grotesque and humorous effect.

CHAPTER 7

Der Steppenwolf: *Crisis and Recovery*

I *Years of Crisis Within and Without*

THE novel *Steppenwolf* (1927) is, in some respects, Hesse's greatest achievement in that genre. It reflects a major crisis not only in the author's thinking and feeling but in the external world as it appeared to him; and the work is a *tour de force* in literary form and structure. But the autobiographical aspects are even more directly revealed in three other works which immediately preceded the novel.

The earliest of these, *Kurgast* (*Spa Visitor*), originally printed in a limited edition under the title *Psychologia Balnearia* (*Notes on a Cure in Baden*, 1924), is a self-analysis, outwardly of Hesse's reactions to a four-week cure in the mineral waters of Baden in Switzerland, but inwardly of his role as a writer, as an outsider, and of his position vis-à-vis the others (the "child-people" of *Siddhartha*, the bourgeois of *Der Steppenwolf*).

The outward circumstances of Hesse's life at this time reflect his awareness of himself as an "outsider," a denizen of the "steppe" (both terms occur in *Kurgast* as well as *Steppenwolf*).[1] His first marriage was legally terminated by divorce in 1923—the same year in which, by acquiring Swiss citizenship, he severed his ties with his German fatherland. The initial enthusiasm and productivity of the first years in Montagnola had given way to brooding doubt, and this extended to the political and cultural situation of Germany in particular and of Western Europe in general. Hesse was approaching fifty, and *Der Steppenwolf* has been regarded as mirroring the crisis which this milestone may precipitate in a man's life. On medical advice, for the treatment of sciatica, he made his first visit to the spa hotel Verenahof in the spring of 1923 and returned—always to the same room (which is still pointed out to visitors)—each year for the next two decades. In 1925 he began to spend part of every winter in Zürich occupying a small apartment in the Schanzengraben provided for him by his friends Alice and Fritz Leuthold. Here he saw something of the café life pictured in *Der Steppenwolf*.

In January, 1924, Hesse married Ruth Wenger, the daughter of the Swiss authoress Lisa Wenger. (She had appeared in *Klingsor* under the guise of the "queen of the mountains" dwelling in the parrot house in Carona.) The marriage lasted only a few months and was officially terminated by divorce in 1927. There are direct references to the relationship in the "crisis" poems, but indirectly the unsuccessful second marriage underlies the pessimistic soul searching of these years.

Kurgast begins by juxtaposing the "outsider" patient, Hesse, with the others. This culminates in a battle fought inwardly against "the Dutchman" in the adjoining room—a character whose attributes suggest Thomas Mann's Klöterjahn, bursting with "normal" bourgeois vitality:

Most of all I noted the innumerable signs of his strength, health, and irrepressibility, his laughter, his good humor, the energy of his movements, the superior detachment of his look, all these symptoms of his biological and social superiority. . . . Vaguely I was reminded of the Flying Dutchman—had he not also been a cursed demon and tormenting spirit? (IV, 62–63)

The hero's brooding upon his attitude to the Dutch occupant of the adjoining room brings him to reflect on his favorite theme of unity:

I believe in nothing . . . so deeply, no other idea is so sacred to me as that of oneness, the idea that the whole of the world is a divine

unit and that all suffering, all evil consists in the fact that we individuals no longer feel ourselves indissoluble parts of the whole, and
that the ego takes itself too seriously. I had endured much suffering
in my life, had done much wrong, had got myself into much that
was stupid and bitter, but over and over again I had succeeded in
redeeming myself, in forgetting and surrendering my ego, in feeling
oneness, in recognizing as illusory the cleft between the internal and
the external, between self and world, and with shut eyes willingly
entering into oneness. (IV, 63–64)

This brings him to the solution: "If I succeeded in loving him,
then all his health, all his vitality would no longer help him,
then he would be mine, then his image no longer opposed the
thought of oneness" (IV, 66). He succeeds in creating within
himself a new lovable image of the hated Dutchman but, ironically, his victory is short-lived since the object of his intense
struggle vacates the room on the next day.

The following chapter "Missmut" ("Moodiness") serves to
extend the theme to the whole environment. Typical attributes
of the twentieth century serve to focus the hero's antipathy: the
cinema, trivial music, gambling, the cult of work and money.
Through this train of thought he arrives at a broader solution.
The crazy world we live in becomes bearable—even lovable—if
we cultivate humor and regard life as a game. He is inclined to
regard his "linguistic experiments" to express this as failures
and laments that he is not a musician:

If I were a musician, I could write without difficulty a two-voice
melody, a melody consisting of two lines, of two rows of notes and
tones which correspond and complement each other, confront and
determine each other, but which at each moment, at every point in
the series, stand in the most intimate lively reciprocity and mutual
relationship. . . . Well, it is just this two-part melody and this
eternally progressing antithesis, this double line that I would like
to express with my material—with words—and I work myself sore
at it but it is no go. (IV, 113)

Der Steppenwolf, however, was to become Hesse's triumph
in developing this counterpoint technique. Meanwhile, this
glimpse into *Kurgast,* one of his most personal books, reveals the
effort, the self-doubt, the despair which preceded the triumph.

Two years later, Hesse allowed himself to be tempted out of
his lair, his "steppe," to undertake a brief lecture tour in South

Der Steppenwolf

German cities. This brought him to further reflections in *Die Nürnberger Reise* (*Trip to Nuremberg*, 1925). He cannot understand why the public should pay to hear a "little poet" read for an hour from his works. His problem is basically that he has no confidence in the importance of his works or in the whole literature of his age. His skepticism rests, he declares,

in my distrust of literature in general. . . . I do not believe in the value of the literature of our age. To be sure, I perceive that every age must have its literature, just as it must have its politics, its ideals, its fashions. But I cannot escape the conviction that the German literature of our age is an ephemeral and dubious affair, seed grown on thin, badly tilled soil, interesting of course and full of problems but hardly capable of mature, full, long-lasting results. Consequently, I can only feel the attempts of contemporary German writers (my own included, of course) as somehow inadequate, imitative and decadent. . . . On the other hand, I see the value of a literature of transition, of a literature that has become problematical and unsure, in the fact that it expresses its own plight and the plight of the age confessionally and with the utmost sincerity. (IV, 155–56)

This Hesse has endeavored to do, and *Steppenwolf* does express the author's self-doubt and torment, and that of our age as well.

The further conclusion affirms that reached in *Kurgast*, namely the necessity of "humor, the old mediator between ideal and reality" (IV, 158). *Die Nürnberger Reise* shows a greater tendency, on Hesse's part, to view himself and the surrounding world in a mildly humorous light. But not until *Der Steppenwolf* itself does this humor show its full development resting on the grotesque juxtaposition of the ideal and the real. This basis of humor has a certain affinity with the Romantic irony of E.T.A. Hoffmann and Jean Paul (whose *Badereise des Doktors Katzenberger* is mentioned in the preface to the *Kurgast*).

The third work related to the *Steppenwolf* novel is the cycle of poems called *Krisis* which was published in a limited edition in 1928. But a number of these poems (including "Besoffener Dichter" below) were printed, before the appearance of the novel, in *Die Neue Rundschau* (1926, II, pp. 509–521), under the title "Der Steppenwolf: Ein Stück Tagebuch in Versen." This title—"A Diary Fragment in Verses"—points to the subjective, autobiographical element in the material from which the novel grew.

Few of these poems were taken into the collected works. They are deliberately shocking and are written mainly in *Knüttelvers* (doggerel verse). By the use of this form Hesse turns his back upon estheticism and bares his soul, as Faust does with his "existential" questioning of the meaning of life in his opening monologue. In "Besoffener Dichter" ("Drunken Poet") we read:

> Bald, wenn ich wieder betrunken bin,
> Kommt ein Automobil gerannt,
> Der karrt mich zu Tode mit sicherer Hand,
> Hoffentlich bricht auch er dabei das Genick,
> Dieser glückliche Katholik,
> Besitzer von Haus, Fabrik und Garten,
> Auf den zwei Kinder und eine Gattin warten
> Und der noch mehr Geld verdient hätte und Kinder gezeugt,
> Wenn nicht ein besoffener Dichter
> Ihm gelaufen wäre zwischen die Auto-Lichter.[2]

The reader cannot fail to miss the note of sardonic humor which serves as a counterpoint to the pessimism regarding the poet's situation and the bourgeois values of the surrounding world. Nor is the reader likely to miss the allusion to the war on automobiles in *Steppenwolf*. One further example from these poems will have to suffice. "Mit diesen Händen . . ." reveals the identity of the author and the "Steppenwolf," referring to the "murder" of Hermine in the Magic Theater under the name of Hesse's second wife:

> Alles lässt mich im Stich,
> Jetzt ist auch meine Liebe kaputt.
> Es war so schauerlich,
> Sie hiess Erika Maria Ruth.
> Lang lauschte ich an ihren offenen Lippen,
> Da kam kein Hauch und kein Ton!
> Und kein Herzschlag unter den Rippen,
> Es war alles aus und entflohn.
> Nun gibt es keinen Streit und keine Liebe mehr,
> O ich verlorener Sohn,
> Auch diese Blume hab' ich gebrochen;
> Alles ist leer,
> Ich wollt, ich wär tot, ich wollt, ich wär
> Das Messer, mit dem ich sie totgestochen.

Der Steppenwolf

> Das Blut am Boden war schwarz geronnen,
> Lang blieb ich darin stehn;
> Doch von all den erloschenen Sonnen
> War kein Abendrot mehr, kein Schimmer zu sehn.
> Ich habe sie vom Himmel gerissen
> Und mit meinen Händen zu Scherben geschmissen,
> So musste es enden,
> Mit diesen bleichen blutigen Händen. . . .[2]

In a postscript, Hesse points out that these verses are by no means solely concerned with the tragicomedy of the fifty-year-old but deal with "one of those stages in life in which *Geist* becomes tired of itself, dethrones itself and gives way to nature, chaos, the sensual. In my life, periods of intense sublimation and of asceticism striving for spiritualization have always alternated with periods of surrender to the naive, the sensuous, the childlike, to foolishness, even craziness and danger. Everyone has this within him." This oscillation is strikingly apparent in the four major works of this period. *Demian* shows marked affinity with *Der Steppenwolf* while the intervening *Siddhartha* more closely resembles *Narziss und Goldmund* (1930).

II *Perspectives*

The re-issue, twenty years later, of Basil Creighton's unsatisfactory translation of *Der Steppenwolf* was greeted by *Time* (March 17, 1947) as "a repellent example of that beery old thing, German Romanticism, being sick in the last ditch before Naziism." The reviewer continued: "The end of his madness is not suicide but murder." Here, of course, the reviewer revealed his complete lack of understanding of the symbolic planes of action.

The work has puzzled many readers, some of whom wrote to the author to express their shocked indignation. Hesse's published letters contain a number of exhortations not to overlook the other spiritual dimensions of the work. A variety of interpretations have been offered, but most critics, from the beginning, perceived the importance of the theme and structure of the novel. Almost simultaneously with *Time*'s uncomprehending condemnation, Thomas Mann wrote in an introduction to the American reprint of *Demian* that in *Steppenwolf* Hesse had succeeded in creating a novel whose form was unprecedented.[4]

Hesse was well aware of the dilemma of the contemporary novel when he stated:

We novelists of today are carrying on an art that belongs to the day after tomorrow, an art whose laws and forms do not yet exist. It will be an art which is no longer the representation of events and relationships, but only the revelation of the inner psychic realm of a single isolated human being.[5]

This could stand as a programmatic statement of Hesse's aim in writing *Steppenwolf*, which cannot be judged by criteria applied to the traditional realistic novel. Ziolkowski, has called its structure a "sonata in prose"[6] in which a musical counterpoint develops between a "realistic" stratum or linear development and a deliberately "unreal" (psychological or metaphysical) melody tied in a contrapuntal relation to the story line. Much of the humor depends on this sometimes incongruous juxtaposition. A kind of double vision or double perspective is attained, and this provides the basis of ironic humor.

III *Plot and Themes*

In the novel, the hero (or anti-hero) Harry Haller is examined from three perspectives. He is introduced through his bourgeois landlady's nephew, who writes by way of introduction what little he knows of this strange man whose papers he purports to be editing. The main body of the book consists of the first-person narration of Haller, which is interrupted by the insertion of a thirty-page "objective" psychoanalysis—the "Tract"—which, in the original edition, was paginated separately and printed in different type on yellow paper.

Haller is at odds with himself and the world. At fifty he approaches the end of middle age, foreseeing future decline and death. He contemplates suicide but is saved from this fate by meeting Hermine, who introduces him to the side of life hitherto shunned by him, to pleasures of the senses, dancing, jazz, and sex. This one-sided intellectual thus discovers another dimension in life. Haller has habitually regarded himself as a "lone wolf"—an outsider—who sees life as a dichotomy in which *Bürgertum* (bourgeois values and attitudes) stands at one

pole and the artist-intellectual at the other. This self-characteri-
zation is shown to be oversimplified. The "Tract" develops the
theme of manifold potential personalities inherent in the individual. This is suggestive of Jung's emphasis on multiple factors in personality versus Freud's single emphasis on sexuality.

Harry Haller (how could it be otherwise in Hesse's subjective
works?) is an artist, a writer. This facet, however, is played down
in favor of the aging outsider-intellectual theme. Nevertheless,
we are informed that Haller has written and published much,
and we have the first-person narration of Haller's "Notes,"
including several poems—"Ich Steppenwolf trabe und trabe"
(IV, 252) and "Die Unsterblichen" (IV, 348–49, 407)—which
form part of *Krisis* and, therefore, enhance the identification
of Haller with his creator.

On the plane of pseudo-reality, the story brings Haller out of
his ivory-tower intellectualism and into contact with sensual
pleasures. Hermine sends an even more versatile sexual partner,
Maria, to his bed. But this is only the bass counterpoint line to
the development of the surreal elements of the book, culminating in the Magic Theater. The symbol of the mirror, after
many leitmotif allusions, is now used to show Haller, in a passage of sustained surrealism, the multiple facets of his personality and the many possibilities of development. The life of
sensual enjoyment is only one of these. At the same time, the
motif of homosexuality is used to show the innate bisexuality
of human beings. Instead of life being a simple dichotomy
between male and female principles, both exist in countless
combinations and proportions in everyone.

The Magic Theater subsumes all the major motifs and themes
which had been introduced earlier. To trace the homosexual
motif, we may recall that Hermine reminds Haller of his boyhood friend Hermann. In the feminine counterpart of Hesse's
own name there is a double allusion. At the masquerade ball,
Hermine is dressed as a boy and finally attracts Haller in this
disguise. Pablo urges a sexual orgy *à trois* which Haller, inhibited
by bourgeois moral conventions, indignantly declines. In the
Magic Theater, while looking into Pablo's magic mirror (a deliberate parodistic fairy-tale allusion), Haller sees two reflections of
himself: an elegant young man embracing Pablo and going off
with him, while a charming youth of sixteen or seventeen dashes
down the corridor to a booth marked "All Girls Are Yours!"

This is only one of the themes recapitulated in the Magic Theater. Others—humor, music, criticism of technology and nationalism—will be discussed in the following sections.

IV *Humor*

Obviously there is an element of humor in the grotesque exaggerations of these surreal dream-world projections into the realm of mundane reality. Humor comes more to the fore in the bizarre reflection of Haller's participation in the war on automobiles, alongside his boyhood friend Gustav, who has meanwhile become a professor of theology. In Haller, as in every man, lies the potential killer. Exulting after shooting down his first automobile, Haller exclaims "Funny that shooting is such fun. And to think I used to be a pacifist!" (IV, 382).

Haller sees automobiles on the streets, some of them armored, hunting down pedestrians, running over them, reducing them to pulp. Gustav and Harry pick off alternate autos. In one of these sits a female figure hidden behind a blue veil. This leads Haller to wonder whether the most beautiful woman's face might not be laughing under it. There may be various allusions here: the motif of the quest for the Ideal symbolized in the Romantic blue flower; the motif of the veil that obscures the meaning of life and the nature of the ideal; and the ubiquitous motif of laughter. The next words in the text plainly hint at the unreal nature of the action: "Good Lord, if we were playing robbers . . . it would have been nicer not to extend our murderous impulses to pretty ladies" (IV, 377). This is just what Haller does in the climactic scene of the Magic Theater, when he plunges an imagined knife into an imagined figure of Hermine lying in the embrace of Pablo.

Besides its richly grotesque humor, the episode of the war on automobiles illustrates that instinctive murderous traits lurk even in the outsider-pacifist, in the intellectual Haller-Hesse. At the same time, this surreal dream-war on machines can be regarded as summing up the theme of criticism of contemporary technological civilization which is woven into the texture of the novel, frequently in conjunction with music. For modern music, as well as modern machines, can serve to symbolize the alienation of the individual in the modern world, leading to the development of "mass-man" in terms of Ortega y Gasset's analysis.

The humor here has something in common with the humor of Kafka in *The Metamorphosis* and of the Theater of the Absurd of Ionesco and his followers. Consider the grotesque chivalry of Gustav's approach to the car he has just brought to a halt: "Excuse me, old boy, my name is Gustav. We have just taken the liberty of shooting your chauffeur. May we inquire to whom we have the honor of speaking?" (IV, 379). The occupant turns out to be Attorney-General Loering. He is requested to dismount so that the demolition of the auto may be completed, but he prefers to be demolished with it. Gustav permits himself another question: "It has always been incomprehensible to me how anyone can be a state attorney. You live by accusing others, mostly poor devils, and obtaining a verdict of guilty. Don't you?" The attorney replies that it was his duty, his office and "anyway, you kill too." Gustav rejoins: "Correct. Only we don't kill out of duty but for pleasure. Or rather for displeasure, out of despair about the world. Therefore killing is sort of fun for us."

Later, after another auto has bit the dust, Gustav remarks with a smile: "Yes, there are just too many people in the world. Formerly it wasn't as noticeable. But now when everyone wants not merely to breathe but to have an automobile as well, one just can't help noticing it." It is remarkable that this was written in 1926 when the automotive industry was in its infancy. But perhaps the observation was more humorous then than it is now when the grotesque exaggeration shows signs of becoming grim reality.

> V Die Ewigkeit ist bloss ein Augenblick,
> gerade lang genug für einen Spass
> (*Goethe, quoted in* Steppenwolf)

In *Steppenwolf*, humor and the motif of laughter are prominent attributes of the two central figures of Goethe and Mozart, representatives of the "Immortals." Harry dreams that he is in an antechamber waiting for an interview with Goethe. A scorpion repeatedly tries to crawl up his leg. He recognizes the animal as "a beautiful dangerous heraldic symbol of femininity and sin" (IV, 282), and imagines that it is a messenger from

Molly and that its name may be Vulpius. At the end of the interview with Goethe, he asks about Molly. With a laugh Goethe shows him a tiny woman's leg, exquisitely wrought in ivory. As Harry is about to take the leg into his hand, it jerks, and Harry, suspecting that it might be a scorpion, starts back. Goethe, now become very old, laughs quietly and teases him with the little toy, delighting in Harry's conflict of desire for the dainty object and his fear of it; whereupon the old man disappears.

This dream clearly expresses Harry Haller's ambivalence with regard to erotic love and suggests how his problem might be solved.[7] Hesse's choice of a scorpion to represent Harry's conception of womanhood and sin is by no means arbitrary. In folklore the scorpion is regarded as "a creature, which has a very tender face to be compared with the countenance of a chaste virgin."[8] Like women, therefore, it has its beauty and innocent charm. At the same time, however, its opposite end is capable of delivering a painful, possibly fatal sting, and the creature is, therefore, to be feared and avoided. Thus the scorpion evokes the same ambivalence and the same "quivering conflict of desire and fear" (IV, 287) in Harry Haller as women like Hermine do.

Folklore also holds that the oil of the scorpion is a cure for the pain of its sting, and the scorpion is, therefore, all the more appropriate as a symbol of the fair sex, for as Beaumont and Fletcher noted: "Women . . . relish much of scorpions,/For both have stings, and both can hurt too."[9] The medicinal property of the scorpion makes it a particularly apt symbol for sexuality in *Der Steppenwolf,* for the book itself is intended as a record of Harry's homeopathic cure. Just as peasants believed that they could still the pain of the scorpion's sting through application of scorpion oil, so it is implied that Harry may overcome his fear of sex through the application of sex.

In its association with Molly and Vulpius, the scorpion hints at precedents for this cure; for by identifying Molly as the subject of Bürger's poems, Hesse makes it clear that he is pointing to the sister of Gottfried August Bürger's first wife, Dorette. Because Bürger loved Molly and not Dorette, the three decided to live together, with Dorette as the poet's wife *de jure* and Molly his wife *de facto.*[10]

Similarly, Christiane Vulpius represents a situation outside of social convention, since her common-law relationship with Goethe was sealed by formal marriage only after eighteen years. Thus both Molly and Vulpius show how the "Immortals" Bürger and Goethe were not confined by society's definition of sin. They enter Harry's dream at this moment as an augury of Harry's liberation from his enslavement to accepted morality.

Hermine begins her cure by diagnosing Harry's illness as excessive idealism. Since reality has never been able to live up to his ideal conceptions, his erotic experiences have all been unhappy: "To love ideally and tragically, my friend, of that you are certainly well capable" (IV, 318). Her advice is that he should not take love so seriously, and she prescribes a light-hearted affair: "You really need to sleep once more with a pretty girl. . . . You will learn now how to love in the usual human way" (IV, 318). She then sends Maria to his bed. Harry's first reaction on discovering the girl is "what would his landlady say!"—a humorous dig at his domination by bourgeois conventional morality.

The somewhat esoteric allusions to the unconventional connubial relations of Bürger and Goethe offer a good example of the degree to which this book, which, in one sense, embraces the sensuous pole, is composed consciously and intellectually.

VI Kulturkritik

Under the guise of the fictitious bourgeois narrator and purported "editor" of Haller's papers, Hesse permits himself some almost specious comments on the age, for Haller's psychosis "is not the idiosyncrasy of an individual but the illness of the epoch itself, the neurosis of that generation to which Haller belongs. . . . Human life becomes real suffering, hell, only when two epochs, two cultures and religions intersect each other" (IV, 205–206). He reports how the Steppenwolf gloated over finding in Novalis (eighty years before Nietzsche), the epigram: "One should be proud of pain—every pain is a reminder of our high calling." Thus it is implied that Haller finds his situation painful in the age and society in which he has to live.

The second page of Haller's papers speaks stridently of "those bad days of inner emptiness and despair in which, amid the destroyed earth, sucked dry by joint stock companies, the world of men and so-called culture grimaces at us" (IV, 208).

Hesse castigates mainly two megalomanias: absurd faith in technological progress and nationalism. The first offers as its special targets gramophones, radios, and automobiles. These increase the tendency toward mechanization of human life and human relationships: "Everything could just as well be done or left undone by machines" (IV, 265). This is followed by the dinner at the professor's house, at which Haller offends his hostess by his violent criticism· of her favorite stereotype portrait of Goethe:

"Let's hope," I said, "that Goethe did not really look like that. This vanity and noble pose, this dignity ogling the respected audience and beneath the manly surface this world of sweetest sentimentality! One can have a lot against him and I too often have a lot against his venerable pomposity. But to depict him thus, no, that goes too far." (IV, 269)

Having shown his fangs in the smug bourgeois milieu, the Steppenwolf runs away to get drunk in a succession of bars, ending up in the Black Eagle, where he meets Hermine. The Goethe portrait in the professor's house suggests the leveling, mechanical, and superficial aspect of bourgeois civilization.

The explosion over the picture of Goethe had been provoked, however, by the professor's nationalist tirade at the journalist who bears the same name as Haller (it *was* Haller) and who has written that Germany's war guilt was in no way inferior to that of the other nations. Hesse is, naturally, referring to his own anti-nationalist writings and their effect. In several passages, he sees another war as the inevitable outcome of nationalistic thinking egged on by a chauvinistic press. As Haller states:

"Several times I have expressed the opinion that every nation and, indeed, every individual, instead of soothing himself with false politi- ~al 'questions of guilt,' should inquire within himself to what degree ᴛhrough mistakes, neglect, and bad habits he shares guilt for the war and for all other human misery. That they cannot forgive me, for naturally they themselves are completely innocent; the Kaiser, the generals, the industrialists, the politicians, the newspapers. . . . One could imagine that everything is magnificent in the world. Only a dozen million dead lie in the earth. . . . Two thirds of my compatriots read such reports day and night . . . and the goal and end of all that is another war, the next war, the coming war, which will be even more horrible than the last." (IV, 307)

From the tone of these passages one could conclude that Hesse was pessimistic concerning the future of the world, whatever the possibilities of individual transcendence. While this is basically true, the pessimism acquires a shade of optimism through the faith in reason (*Geist*) which underlies the whole work. The eternal presence of the Immortals, represented by Novalis and his "golden trace" and by the serene yet gay laughter of Goethe and Mozart, can be interpreted as being symbolic of the eternal potential in man for a better future.

VII *The Meaning of Music*

Music permeates both the form and the content of Hesse's novel. Here we shall examine the meaning of music, postponing our discussion of the formal aspects to the following section. Classical music—represented by Bach and Mozart—symbolizes immortal *Geist,* while jazz represents mainly *Sinnlichkeit* (sensuality). But the aim is to bridge this polarity, and Hesse finds elements in jazz which attract him much more than avant-garde academic music:

Jazz was repugnant to me, but I was ten times more fond of it than of all academic music of today. With its joyous, untamed savagery, it penetrated, even with me, into the sphere of instinct and breathed a naive honest sensuality. . . .

One half of this music, the lyrical part, was "schmalzy," oversweet, dripping with sentimentality, while the other half was wild, moody, and powerful; and yet both halves went together naively and peacefully and produced a whole. It was *Untergangsmusik* (music of decadence); in the Rome of the last emperors there must have been similar music. Naturally, compared with Bach and Mozart and real music, it was disgusting. . . . but . . . this music had the advantage of a great sincerity, of a charming undeceiving primitiveness and of a joyous, childlike mood. It had something of the Negro and something of the American who, in all his strength, seems to us Europeans so boyishly fresh and childlike. (IV, 221)

This passage assigns a multiple role to music. The dichotomy between classical music and jazz symbolizes the dichotomy between Steppenwolf and bourgeois or *Geist* and *Natur* (mind–matter) but more than that, we see in the attraction of jazz the receptiveness of the Steppenwolf for the world of dancing and sex into which he is led by Hermine. Thirdly we see how even jazz prefigures the solution of the wolf–bourgeois cleavage in the capacity of the two components for peaceful coexistence to form a whole. Jazz is *Musik des Untergangs* but contains within itself the seed of a new birth. This train of thought recalls the essay on Dostoyevsky's *Brothers Karamazov:* "This *Untergang* is a return to the world of the mother, it is a return to Asia, to the sources, to the Faustian 'Mothers,' and will, of course, lead to a new birth, like every death on earth" (VII, 162).

On the other hand, Mozart is immortal, ever available and ever present to the individual who will seek him. Even disfigured in such a hellish contraption as the phonograph or radio (the date was 1927), the mind or spirit in Mozart cannot be completely extinguished. It is Mozart himself who, in the Magic Theater, sets up a radio and tunes in to a Munich station broadcasting a concerto grosso of Handel:

To my indescribable amazement and horror, the infernal funnel now spat forth a mixture of bronchial phlegm and chewed rubber which owners of radios and gramophones have agreed to call music—and beneath the murky slime and groans, as if beneath a thick layer of dirt, an exquisite figure, the noble structure of this divine music was recognizable. . . .

"My God," I exclaimed in horror, "what are you doing, Mozart? . . . Are you insisting on letting loose on us this abominable apparatus, the triumph of our age, its last victorious weapon in the war of annihilation against art? Do you have to, Mozart?" (IV, 408)

Mozart laughs and laughs and then comments on the intricate wonders of Handel's composition and points out that all the mechanical, distorting factors in the rendition "nevertheless cannot destroy the *Urgeist* [basic spirit] of this music" (IV, 409). He then continues:

"My dear chap, you are hearing and seeing at the same time an excellent symbol of all life. When you listen to the radio, you hear and see the everlasting struggle between idea and appearance,

between eternity and transience, between the divine and the human.
. . . The whole of life is like that, my boy, and we must accept it
and, if we are not asses, laugh at it. . . . Learn to take seriously what
is worth seriousness and laugh at the rest." (IV, 409–410)

The lesson is reinforced when, at the end of the "trip" in the
Magic Theater, Mozart turns out to be Pablo, a saxophone
player and also a drug and sex addict. Thus Hesse implies that
every individual has within him the potentialities which the
spirit of a Mozart is capable of animating, and that the continued existence of such individual Immortals as Goethe and
Mozart is the portent of the undying potentialities inherent in
the individual human soul.

It is significant that Mozart and not Beethoven was the figure
chosen to convey this message.[11] In fact, Hesse sees symptoms of
decadence already setting in with Beethoven and culminating in
Brahms and Wagner. In a passage near the end, Mozart brings
the theme of music into conjunction with humor as he conjures
up an amusing vision of Wagner and Brahms condemned to
Sisyphean labors. We are transported to a vast desert ringed by
misty mountains and the sea:

In this plain we saw a dignified old bearded gentleman who, with
melancholy mien, was leading a mighty procession of some tens of
thousands of men clothed in black. It looked depressing and hopeless,
and Mozart said:
"Look, that's Brahms. He's striving for redemption, but he still
has a good way to go."
I learned that the thousands of black figures were all the players
of those voices and notes which, according to divine judgment, had
been redundant in his scores.
"Instrumentation too turgid, too much material squandered,"
Mozart nodded.
And immediately afterwards we saw Richard Wagner marching at
the head of an equally great host and felt the heavily laden
thousands pulling and drawing on him; we saw him, too, drag him-
self along on tired, contrite feet. . . .
Mozart laughed. ". . . Turgid instrumentation was after all neither
Wagner's nor Brahms's personal shortcoming, it was an error of their
time."
"What? And for that they have to do such heavy penance now?"
I cried accusingly.
"Naturally. It's the normal course of justice. Only when they have

expiated the guilt of their age will it be evident whether there is left a large enough personal contribution to merit a balancing of accounts." (IV, 402–403)

From this passage it is evident that Hesse was highly critical of the mass effects and emotional saturation achieved by means of too full and too elaborate a harmonic emphasis. This is the dangerous, demonic, emotional side of music which he sees suppressing the *Geist* (the spiritual and intellectual qualities), the strictly controlled and yet magically effective pattern of counterpoint melody as exemplified by eighteenth-century and earlier masters. The passage also indicates the reciprocal relationship between the decadent music of Wagner and Brahms and the decadent culture in which they lived, for they could not escape their own time. Thirdly we see that the individual, although powerless so far as the tendency of his time is concerned, is nevertheless involved in guilt for the faults of his generation. The wording even suggests a connection with the religious doctrine of the fall of man. Finally, the passage expresses Hesse's characteristic optimistic faith on an individual plane. Just as Brahms and Wagner can work their way out of the purgatory they have created for themselves, so can the individual work his way through the layers of impediments in the surrounding world and arrive at a genuine expression of his latent personality as he responds to the manifestations of *Geist*.

Since humor plays such an important part, it may not be altogether irrelevant before leaving this passage to refer to the following paragraphs. The vision of the predicament of Wagner and Brahms provokes in Hesse—or rather in his hero Harry Haller—a nightmare spectacle in which he, too, is condemned to drag thousands upon thousands of similar black figures after him: all those words he had written that were superfluous, all the typesetters and their hours of futile toil, the labors of proofreaders, and the wasted time of readers.

VIII *Musical Form*

Many readers wrote to Hesse complaining about the discordant, unpleasant aspects of his *Steppenwolf*. In his replies, Hesse pointed out that the themes and problems dealt with were not "nice": memories of war and fears of the coming war,

Der Steppenwolf

"jazz and cinema and your whole daily life, whose hell you don't want to allow the author to depict" (VII, 495). Occasionally, these letters claim for this novel the attributes of strict musical form: "From a purely artistic point of view, *Steppenwolf* is at least as good as *Goldmund*. It is constructed around the intermezzo of the tractate just as strictly and rigidly as a sonata and develops its theme neatly" (VII, 495). This gave Ziolkowski the starting point and the title for his interpretation "The Steppenwolf: A Sonata in Prose." [12] Here we can do no more than refer to the main points of his argument.

Ziolkowski sees the three "movements" of the sonata to consist of (a) the preliminary material, (b) "the action," (c) "the so-called 'Magic Theater'":

> The preliminary material, in turn, has three subdivisions: the introduction, the opening passages of Haller's narrative, and the "Tract." These three subdivisions do not constitute part of the action or plot of the novel; they are all introductory in nature. This fact distinguishes them from the second and longest part of the book, which tells the story and which alone of the three main sections has a form roughly analogous to the structure of the conventional novel. . . . The third section, finally, sets itself apart from the bulk of the novel by virtue of its fantastic elements: it belongs, properly speaking, to the action of the novel, for it depicts a situation that takes place in the early hours of the day following the final scene of the plot, and there is no technical division whatsoever. But the conscious divorce from all reality separates this section from the more realistic narrative of the middle part. [13]

The first section presents three thematic developments of Haller's soul as viewed from the perspective of the *Bürger,* of the Steppenwolf himself, and of the author or authors of the "Tract"—and these can be none other than the Immortals, "for no one else could have this lofty and all-encompassing view of the world."

> The introduction states the two themes; the second section brings the development . . .; and the "Tract" recapitulates the themes theoretically and proposes a resolution of the conflict. This scheme, exposition–development–recapitulation, can be found in any book on music under the heading "sonata-form" or "first-movement form," for it is the classical structure for the opening section of the sonata. . . .
> The exposition states two themes with one in the tonic, the other

in the dominant; the development follows in which the potentialities of these themes are worked out; and the recapitulation restates the themes as they occurred in the exposition, but this time both are in the tonic, and the conflict has been resolved.

In the novel the difference in keys is approximated by the contrasting attitudes of Harry Haller as Steppenwolf, on the one hand, and as *Bürger*, on the other: the first represents, as it were the tonic, and the second the dominant.[14]

The second "movement" or main body of the novel is characterized by counterpoint which achieves a simultaneity or concomitance. Hesse here achieves what, in the passage at the end of *Kurgast*[15] he lamented as being impossible in the medium of words. Ziolkowski illuminates his argument here with detailed references to E.T.A. Hoffmann—especially his novella *Der goldene Topf* which anticipates Hesse's use of double perspective, for the essence of Hoffmann's art in this "Märchen aus der neuen Zeit" (modern fairytale) is the constant interaction of real and surreal elements, the double perspective which simultaneously sees each event from different viewpoints. Ziolkowski may carry his argument a shade too far when he asserts that "Hermine, Pablo, Maria and the entire demimonde of *The Steppenwolf* exist on a realistic plane consistently throughout the book."[16] But he almost convinces us by adding that "only Haller's sense of double perception bestows upon them the added dimension by which they assume symbolic proportions." One may question whether this explanation satisfies the reader who must feel bewildered by Hermine's frequent excursions into aspects of philosophy, literature, and psychoanalysis which seem to disqualify her as a "call-girl" existing on the plane of reality. It seems to me it is equally possible to view her and the other characters as constantly flitting in and out of the real and surreal worlds—like Hoffmann's creation, who is at one moment an archivist, and at the next a salamander.

At any rate, the use of the terms "counterpoint" and "double perspective" is helpful in analyzing the nature of the development of this second "movement," in which "we find an extended narrative that consciously exploits the technique of double perception—a device . . . that Hesse explicitly conceived in musical terms as the literary equivalent of counterpoint. In this section the themes of the first movement—Haller's notion of polarity between Steppenwolf and *Bürger,* as well as the broader view of reality and illusion—are skilfully developed with constant interplay and reciprocity." [17]

The third movement is seen as a "Finale: Theme with Variations." On the realistic plane, no more than a fantasy induced by narcotics—today one would say an LSD trip—the "Magic Theater" actually recapitulates all the themes and motifs of the novel:

In retrospect the structure of the Magic Theater emerges as a theme with variations. The theme, borrowed from the "Tract," is the notion that Haller's personality comprises a multiplicity of opposite elements. . . . For the duration of the Magic Theater—until the murder of Hermine's image—he observes life from a point outside the polar sphere of the *Bürger,* and he is able to accept all its aspects. Each booth in the Magic Theater represents a variation on this theme: in each one he sees a specific instance of the opposite tendencies in his nature, and yet he affirms all of them completely. [18]

In no other work—including the *Glasperlenspiel,* where music carries the main theme—has Hesse used musical forms with more subtlety and skill as the main structural element.

IX *Goethe and the* Bildungsroman

In his discussion of *Der Steppenwolf,* Egon Schwarz has pointed to parallels with Goethe's Faust. [19] At the beginning of the action, both protagonists are men beyond the prime of life who have assimilated the academic and cultural *Bildung* of their time; in both, this intellectual achievement leaves only nausea and leads to the contemplation of suicide; both are preserved from self-destruction by the intervention of a supersensory being with whom they make a pact concerning forbidden things; both are led to that realm of experience to which they have been strangers: Auerbach's Cellar corresponds to Harry Haller's bars; the love relationship between Haller and Maria reminds us of Faust and Gretchen; and the great masquerade ball suggests the Walpurgis Night.

Yet with all these parallels and possible allusions, Hesse's composition is no imitative work of decadence. Even the relationship of this novel to the German tradition of the *Bildungs-*

roman is unique, for, as Schwarz suggests, *Der Steppenwolf* can
be seen as a *Bildungsroman* turned upside down. In this sense,
it culminates the development begun with Goethe's *Wilhelm
Meister*. With the nobility gone and the bourgeoisie in a late
stage of dissolution, the cultural legacy is revealed as highly
problematic. Harry Haller has acquired what it offered; love and
marriage lie behind this aging man and have been emptied of
all meaning. He must relearn and forget the attitudes stamped
upon him by the cultural environment. He must recapture a lost
wholeness and openness, and he must be made receptive to the
teaching of the Immortals. This involves not *Bildung* but
Rückbildung, i.e., development in reverse. Even in this age of
mass man and mass wares, the immortal aspects of *Geist* symbolized by Goethe and Mozart are omnipresent. It is Mozart who
teaches the lesson that even the mechanical and distorted
medium of the radio cannot obliterate the divine *Geist* inherent
in the musical form. But this is the insight of Goethe's Faust
when he proclaims "Am farbigen Abglanz haben wir das Leben"
("We live by the colored reflection of things").

X *The Triadic Pattern and the Chiliastic Vision*

From what has been said so far, there can be little doubt
about the interpretation of the ending of *Der Steppenwolf*
offered here. Whether the "Magic Theater" be regarded as a
poetic vision, as hallucination produced by narcotics, or as a
form of psychoanalysis—and it is all three simultaneously on
different levels—it is clear, by the reflected or imaginary murder
of Hermine, that Harry Haller has failed. In the first interpretation he may be said to have failed to sustain the poetic vision.
In the second he emerges prematurely from the narcotic dream
and attempts to act on the plane of reality. In the third he
refuses to recognize the emanations proceeding from his own
psyche.

But the failure is heralded as a step on the right path, and the
ending is optimistic. For the pseudo-murder he is condemned to
life by Pablo-Mozart:

"You want to die, you coward, and not live. What the devil! You
shall live, damn it! . . . You shall live and you shall learn to laugh.
You shall learn to listen to the cursed radio music of life, shall

respect the *Geist* beneath it and learn to laugh at the tingle-tangle in it. . . . But I must say, Harry, I'm a little disappointed in you. You have committed a bad blunder. You broke through the humor of my little theater and committed a beastly act; you stabbed with knives and sullied our pretty visionary world." (IV, 413–14)

Multiple allusions are present here. Haller had within him too much conventional morality to stomach the sight of Hermine in Pablo's embrace. But he also had too little *Geist* to sustain the vision and laugh at the failure of the vision to sustain itself in reality, for he had an ideal vision of Hermine (whose frequently learned conversations may be regarded as projections from Haller's own mind) and in reality she is a high-class prostitute whose surrender to Pablo is perfectly natural and "realistic."

Haller has profited from the experience, and the last lines of the novel point optimistically to the future: "One day I would play the game of figures better. One day I would learn laughter. Pablo was awaiting me. Mozart was awaiting me."

In Haller's progress, a triadic pattern may be detected which is curiously different from that of Demian and Siddhartha. In *Demian,* Hesse remained closer to the traditional pattern, believing in spiritual rebirth not only of the individual but of all of humanity. *Siddhartha* represents a shift to distant times and concentrates on one individual whose third stage—or Third Kingdom—is in many respects an Eastern quietism, a blending of mind and matter, soul and body.

Steppenwolf reverses the usual order of the stages of mind and matter. Haller has had to unbutton the straightjacket of preconceived rationalizations and develop the neglected sensual side of his nature. But this is only a step in the progress toward the third stage. In Ziolkowski's words, "By a seeming paradox, it is the prostitute Hermine and the jazz musician Pablo . . . who are the prophets of the Third Kingdom. The sustaining hope of these outsiders, as Hermine informs Harry Haller, is not the bourgeois desire for posthumous fame":[20]

It is not fame, oh no! But what I call eternity. The pious call it God's Kingdom. I think that all of us more demanding individuals with yearning, with one dimension too many, could not live at all, if beyond the atmosphere of this world there was not another to

breathe, if beyond time eternity did not exist and that is the realm of the genuine. . . . In eternity there is no posterity, only coexistence. . . . It is the realm beyond time and appearance. That's where we belong, that's the direction in which our hearts are striving, Steppenwolf, and that's why we yearn for death. There you will find your Goethe again and your Novalis and your Mozart. (IV, 345–46)

We have already commented on the deliberate transcendence of the conventions of realism in the novel in placing such utterances in the mouth of a character such as Hermine. Such dialogues are transpositions from the mind of Haller. But here the point to be made is that the ending of *Steppenwolf*, although embracing multiple interpretations, including the lesson of laughter, strongly emphasizes the role of *Geist* symbolized in the Immortals. It is true that Haller learns to laugh, but humor is a *modus vivendi* to make life bearable. The more basic point is the eternal presence of *Geist*, toward which man is to strive and which points the way.

An inconsistency in the work may be seen in the total divorce of the Immortals from sensory experience. As Boulby declares, "we are forced to take account of the fact that the world these Immortals inhabit is totally beyond the sensual. . . . The depersonalized, though they may treasure ladies' legs in caskets, must find sense experience rather difficult of access." [21]

In many ways, *Der Steppenwolf* marks a crisis and recovery in Hesse's development. Paradoxically, in spite of the spicy sexuality of much of the material, the book is the opposite of pornographic and marks a definite turn toward a more ascetic intellectual pole. It points beyond *Narziss and Goldmund* to *Die Morgenlandfahrt* and *Das Glasperlenspiel*, which stand under the aegis of *Geist*.

CHAPTER 8

Narziss und Goldmund: *Mind,*
Matter—and Art

I *Theme*

B asic in the thematic complex of *Der Steppenwolf,* as we
have seen, was the dichotomy between the ideal and reality
portrayed as hostile principles warring within the psyche of a
single character, Haller. In *Narziss und Goldmund,* the basic
theme is the cleavage between *Geist* and *Natur* (mind and
matter). But these principles are symbolized in the two figures
joined equally in the title. They are not at odds because the one
is the necessary complement of the other, and the intermediary
between the two spheres is art—which is sometimes seen as
belonging to a third intermediate realm of *Seele* (soul).[1] *Der
Steppenwolf,* too, had approached this view of art in the exhortations of Mozart on the radio music of life.

In *Narziss und Goldmund* we have a *Künstlerroman* (artist
novel) reminding us of *Gertrud* and *Rosshalde;* but the comparison reveals Hesse's greater maturity in the later work. His
choice of sculpture as the artistic medium contributes to the precision and plasticity of the confrontation, in contrast with the
diffuse musicality of *Gertrud.* Of all the arts, sculpture most
directly represents the struggle to produce form out of matter.

II *Reception and Historical Considerations*

In *Narziss und Goldmund,* the stridency of *Steppenwolf* is replaced by a rhythmic, harmonious flow reminiscent of the style of *Siddhartha;* and this has been one factor in the enormous popularity of this novel, although its piquant eroticism is perhaps a more important one.

By 1962, nearly a quarter of a million copies had been sold in the Fischer and Suhrkamp single editions alone,[2] without counting the numerous other licensed editions and translations, including the German book-of-the-month club, Büchergilde Gutenberg. This is more than double the sales for any other work by Hesse. The reverse is true in America, where *Steppenwolf* has been Hesse's best seller. In part this may be attributed to the meaningless title given to the first American edition of *Narziss und Goldmund: Death and the Lover.* The reissue as *Goldmund* helped little, since the absence of the second protagonist in the title still encourages a wrong approach.

It is curious how widely disparate associations may be conjured up by the same name. In Günter Grass's *The Dog Years,* "Goldmund" alludes to Eddie Amsel's gold-capped teeth after they had all been smashed by Nazi Storm Troopers. The name, therefore, has almost the same ring as the English "Gold Mouth." Hesse's Goldmund, on the other hand, carries different connotations, suggestive of Mephisto's words in *Faust:* "Grau, teurer Freund, ist alle Theorie,/Und grün des Lebens goldner Baum."[3] The name is also a translation of St. John Chrysostomos "who for inspiration turned to the populace, who did not commune within himself but lived in constant intercourse with his environment."[4] If Goldmund is thus the extrovert, the name Narziss indicates the introvert who cuts himself off from the world and withdraws into himself. The monastery, too, is an apt symbol of the self-contained world of the spirit.

Whereas the German reading public left no doubt as to its preference, the critics have been at odds on the merits of this work.[5] Misunderstanding may lie at the root of both censure and encomia. In the mass of readers and in some critics, the mellifluous and lyric fluency of the narrative has no doubt led to the view that a kind of contrapuntal "harmony" is established between mind and matter, between spirit and life represented in the dual protagonists: "The friendship between Narziss and Goldmund, symbol of a reconciliation of *Geist* and *Leben,* already heralds that harmony presented in its perfection by Leo, the Traveler to the East." [6] We shall see how remote this popular view is from the deeper meaning.

Another approach is taken by Ziolkowski who, by titling his chapter "A Medieval Allegory," has given undue importance to the historical milieu, and Rose echoes this when he states that the book "brings the world of the late Middle Ages vividly alive." [7]

It seems to me that the temporal and geographical setting plays almost as little part in the action as does the legendary Indian world of *Siddhartha.* The external environment is there, and now and then specific medieval elements, such as the Black Death and the rule of the Prince-Bishop, come to the fore. But even such references cannot serve to date this world with any precision. Hesse's approach is rather the opposite of that of the historical novelist. He is not intent on portraying the historical past, nor even on probing the mind of man in a given historical period. Rather he is concerned with portraying himself, the polarities in his own psyche and the network of associated problems. The vague medieval background merely serves to isolate the thematic complex, as did the legendary realm in *Siddhartha.* As Anni Carlsson puts it: "The restrictive embrace of space and time is dissolved in *eternal* Middle Ages and in a broad, loosely conceived German Empire" (italics mine). [8]

Because of his inherent antipathy to the external gadgetry that marks our modern times, it was particularly easy for Hesse to depict the medieval scene without inadvertent anachronisms. Moreover, the description of the monastery and the life of its inmates came naturally to one who had been—however briefly —himself a *Klosterschüler* (monastic pupil or seminarist) in the cloisters of Maulbronn, on which Narziss' Mariabronn is closely modeled, even down to the tree at the entrance. In fact, the gentle scholarly life with its little comforts—and its stress on the study of Greek—is a truer reflection of the monastery in Hesse's time than it was in the fourteenth century when, we are now told by local officials, the Cistercian novitiates and monks died at an average age of twenty-one, mostly of pulmonary infections contracted in the winter. It is situated fourteen hundred feet above sea level on the northerly slope of the

Black Forest, so that the winters are severe; and the Middle Ages had no adequate means of heating the vast complex.

Another factor which throws light on the historical-medieval aspect is the novel fragment *Berthold,* which Hesse wrote in 1907–1908. Since its appearance in print,[9] the critics have drawn parallels with *Narziss und Goldmund.* One fact, however, stands out: the 1907 fragment "points to the intention to write a wholly naturalistic, historical novel. Such a style was not really natural to Hesse; it is questionable whether it was ever in his capacity to create a broad canvas in this mode." [10] He was probably nearer to this approach in the decade in which he translated the medieval Latin of Cäsarius von Heisterbach[11] and composed his most realistic novel *Rosshalde.*

To read the work as a historical novel can lead to misconceptions as to its theme and structure. But let us turn to a survey of the plot.

III *Résumé*

The first six chapters depict the emerging friendship of the *Klosterschüler* Goldmund and the young novice Narziss, whose brilliant intellect has precipitated him into the role of teacher at an age little beyond that of his pupils and even before taking his vows. Goldmund is so attracted to the young preceptor that he is determined to excel in learning and follow his example. Gradually, Narziss leads Goldmund to the awareness that his nature is different and destined for the world. Narziss' function is virtually that of a modern psychoanalyst, as he evokes suppressed memories of Goldmund's gypsy runaway mother. Jungian symbols unite with Bachofen concepts when Narziss elucidates:

"With you Goldmund, *Geist* and *Natur* [mind and matter], consciousness and the dream world, are very disparate. You have forgotten your childhood. From the depths of your soul it is wooing you. . . . Natures like yours, those with strong and delicate senses, full of soul, dreamers, poets, lovers, are almost always superior to us men of intellect. Your origin is maternal. . . . We intellectuals, although we seem frequently to guide and govern you others, do not lead a full life, we live in the wilderness. To you belongs the fullness of life, the garden of love, the beautiful realm of art. Your homeland is the earth, ours the idea. Your danger is drowning in the world of senses, ours suffocation in airless space. You are an artist, I am a thinker. You sleep on the mother's breast, I keep watch in the desert. The sun shines for me, the moon and the stars for you. Your dreams are of girls, mine of boys." (V, 50–51)

Gathering herbs for Brother Anselm, Goldmund is seduced by Lise the gypsy. This precipitates his flight from Mariabronn.

The next ten chapters—the central portion of the novel—cover Goldmund's career in the world. This section has some affinity with the picaresque novel. Goldmund himself, however, is not a picaro since he frequently shows a sentimental streak—in his Romantic love for Lydia and his cherishing of her memory—and a tendency to introspection and moralizing; one example is the encounter with Rebecca, which causes him to question pogroms and massacres and leads him to accuse God of creating an unjust world.

Another element of the picaresque novel, namely humor, is also lacking; and this is surprising in view of Hesse's development of this quality in *Der Steppenwolf*. At least it seems that Hesse's intention was not humorous, although it must be admitted that the narrative precariously balances on the brink of parody, especially in the account of Goldmund's erotic adventures. If Goldmund is not himself a picaro, many of his exploits and adventures are picaresque and other characters, such as Viktor, are typical golliard vagabonds.

As the years pass Goldmund's adventures suggest two related themes: the awareness of transience, especially in the relationship of love and death, and secondly, his awakening to the power of art to stamp eternity on the ephemeral phenomena of the senses.

Goldmund's assistance at childbirth in a peasant cottage reveals to him the relationship between ecstasy and pain: "As he stared with curiosity into the face of the woman in labor . . . something unexpected struck him: the lines in the distorted face of the screaming woman were hardly different from those he had seen on women's faces in the moment of orgasm" (V, 136).

He then joins the renegade cleric Viktor. They wander together for many weeks, until Goldmund is forced to kill his companion in self-defense—and in defense of his gold ducat, which he values not for its monetary worth but, sentimentally, because it was a parting gift from Lydia. Having taken a human life preys upon him and brings him to confess in a church, where he is entranced by a statue of the Virgin. He seeks out its creator, Master Niklaus, whom he persuades to accept him as a pupil. Thus he exchanges a vagabond existence for th esedentary life—temporarily—and finally creates a remarkable figure of the Disciple John in the likeness of Narziss. This artistic achievement induces Niklaus to obtain the guild's consent to issue master's papers and to aspire to Goldmund as son-in-law and heir.

Goldmund feels that now he has nothing within him yearning for creation, and he recoils from the mere routine exercise of his craft. Therefore he returns to the wandering life, but under increasingly gloomy auspices, for he wanders into the Black Death. After many harrowing experiences of love and death—including the encounter with Rebecca, the sole survivor of an assassination of Jews blamed by Christians for the plague—he wanders back to the episcopal city (Cologne is implied but not mentioned by name) seeking Master Niklaus, for his soul is now full of inner visions crying to be engraved in wood, stone, or metal. But it is too late, for Niklaus is dead, and Lisbeth, his daughter, is a deformed and disfigured survivor.

Goldmund catches sight of Agnes, a courtesan of the Imperial Statthalter (administrator—for the Bishop had fled from the plague). He wins her but is discovered *in flagrante delicto* and sentenced to be hanged at dawn. He is allowed a priest for confession and absolution and is determined to kill the priest, if necessary, in order to escape in his vestments. It is Narziss, now Father Johannes and Abbot of Mariabronn, who enters his cell to announce that he has obtained remission of the sentence.

Narziss now plays a leading role in the last four chapters. He provides Goldmund with a studio in the abbey, where Goldmund produces many sculptures and trains an apprentice. But Goldmund is still irresistibly drawn to the nomadic life—and to Agnes. He goes in pursuit of her and finds himself rejected as old and no longer desired. He falls from his horse into a stream, contracting the illness which brings him back to Mariabronn to die. These last adventures are veiled and narrated from Narziss' point of view, piecing together Goldmund's experiences from scraps of information.

Narziss und Goldmund

Narziss reveals how his life has been broadened by his friendship for Goldmund—his only experience of sensual attachment —and by the insight into the nature of art and the creative process. Goldmund's last words echo in his ears: "But how will you ever be able to die, Narziss, if you have no mother? Without a mother one cannot love. Without a mother one cannot die" (V, 322). These words are veiled and elusive, suggesting multiple associations, including Jungian father and mother symbols— animus and anima.[12] One can interpret them in the sense that Narziss cannot "die" because he has not "lived." To live and love, as Goldmund has done, is to become aware of transience, of the presence of death in the midst of the fullness of life, and to ripen toward death.

IV Motifs and Themes

The title *Narziss und Goldmund* gives prominence to the friendship theme, which can be traced through a large part of Hesse's work, from Peter Camenzind and Richard through Hans Giebenrath and Hermann Heilner, Kuhn and Muot, Veraguth and Burkhardt, Siddhartha and Govinda, on to Joseph Knecht and Plinio Dessignori in *Das Glasperlenspiel*.

All of these friendships are of a platonic, spiritual nature. Of Goldmund we read: "Here he was permitted to love, he was allowed to surrender without sin . . . to transform and spiritualize the perilous flames of the senses into noble sacrificial fires" (V, 35). Initiated into psychoanalysis as he was, Hesse was well aware, however, that they represent a sublimation of a basic, possibly unconscious, homo-erotic drive which has its roots in the essential bisexuality of life explored in *Steppenwolf*. Hesse wrote in a letter of 1931:

That these friendships, because they exist between men, are completely free of eroticism is an error. I am sexually "normal" and have never had physical sexual relations with men, but to consider friendships on that account to be completely unerotic seems to me absolutely false. (VII, 508)

In *Narziss und Goldmund* the latent emotional bond is particularly obvious, especially in Narziss' chaste kiss and confession near the end:

Narziss, his heart burning with love and grief, slowly bent down to him, and now he did what he had never done in the many years of their friendship, he touched Goldmund's hair and brow with his lips. . . . "Let me tell you today how much I love you, how much you have always meant to me, how rich you have made my life." (V, 316)

Hesse was no doubt aware also of the frequent presence of a sublimated homo-erotic element in the teacher-pupil relationship. This is one side of a strong didactic tendency in his work. Narziss is not only a friend of almost the same age; he is also a pedagogue, and it is evident that his brillance and success in this capacity stem, in part, from this latent element in his nature and in the situation.

That this undeveloped homosexual component should be present is fitting in view of the variations on the theme of love in Goldmund's life: "Perhaps that was his destiny: to know women and love in a thousand ways and in a thousand varieties to fulfillment, just as many musicians know how to play not only one instrument but three, four, many" (V, 107). Not only does Goldmund experience individual variations of sexuality from peasant to princely paramour, but he also goes through the torment of chaste romantic love with Lydia. It is these encounters of which Deschner is especially critical; and it is hard to believe that Hesse was not himself aware of how close these passages come to parody. But it seems that he was merely intent on covering the whole gamut of erotic relationships.

With Rebecca, the Jewess, Goldmund's advances are rebuffed with scornful disdain, and Goldmund carries eternal memories of his rejection by this proud beauty and of the cruel injustice meted out to her race. Under the Nazi regime, Hesse refused to authorize deletion of these references to barbaric treatment of the Jews, and as a result *Narziss und Goldmund* disappeared from the list of books published in Germany. Yet another kind of love confronts Goldmund in Marie, the crippled daughter of his landlord in the episcopal city, whose forlorn devotion can find satisfaction only in service.

Goldmund's multiple experiences of love coalesce in his artistic vision of the eternal Eva-Mother which embraces love and death in one, and which he hopes to create but which eludes him because "she is unwilling for me to reveal her mystery" (V, 321).

In the sketch "Tessin" in *Bilderbuch* (1926) Hesse wrote:

Narziss und Goldmund

I permit myself with the Madonna a cult of my own and a mythology of my own. In the temple of my religion, she stands beside Venus and Krishna, but as symbol of the soul, as a parable for the living redeeming glow which hovers to and fro between the poles of the world, between *Natur* and *Geist*, igniting the light of love. (III, 896)

This passage illuminates the role of love and of the mother symbol and the mediation of art under the aegis of the "mother."

Water is also used as a leitmotif in this novel. First it occurs in the form of the river, the crossing of which marks the "exemplary event," [13] the flight of Goldmund from Mariabronn. Here we may be reminded of Siddhartha's crossing of the river into the sensual life of the "child-people"; but there are also suggestions of baptism into life, as Goldmund has to immerse himself in order to cross to the other shore. But the symbolism becomes ambivalent and is reversed, in the end, when Goldmund crossing the stream falls into the icy water and embraces the touch of death, reminding us of the repeated drownings occurring in Hesse's works. Since life and death belong together in the world of matter, water partakes of both.

Water is naturally associated with fish, and the dying fish in the market attract Goldmund's attention as often as the living fish at the bottom of the river, whose illusive scintillating shapes suggest the mystery and the beauty of life and death. Water is even more often associated with the mirror motif, which has many functions including that of reflecting the process of transience and decay in Goldmund. But I think a more subtle function of this motif may lie in the indirect allusion to Narziss in those long central chapters in which Goldmund alone holds the stage.

The book has been criticized for its failure to deal equally with the dual protagonists of the title, although Hesse divides the total number of chapters equally, in the sense that Narziss may be said to dominate the first six and closing four while Goldmund alone is present in the intervening ten. But the Goldmund chapters are longer, and he is present throughout the book. Hesse also manages to have Narziss recur in Goldmund's thoughts from time to time; and when Goldmund turns to sculpture, it is the figure of Narziss he is intent on creating. If, however, the Narcissus motif underlies all those water or mirror reflections in Goldmund's vagabondage, then a strengthened claim can be made for the subconscious presence of Narziss during his physical absence.

Just as water embraces the polarities of life and becomes, in a sense, a symbol of oneness, so too Goldmund's diverse erotic experiences coalesce in his artistic vision of the Great Mother:

It is the figure of the great birth-giving primordial mother, and its secret consists not . . . in this or that individual trait, in particular fullness or thinness, robustness or gracefulness . . . but in the fact that the greatest antinomies of the world, ordinarily irreconcilable, have found their peace and dwell together: birth and death, kindness and cruelty, life and annihilation. (V, 190–91)

The figure and the role of the mother can be seen as a further development of the Jungian archetype and the Frau Eva of *Demian.*

Another link with *Demian* can be seen in the recurring theme of *Selbstverwirklichung* (self-realization). Both protagonists find that path of fulfillment appropriate to their different natures, and in the explicit philosophical conversations of the concluding chapters Narziss declares that an individual's efforts to realize himself, using the gifts bestowed on him by nature, represent the highest aim and the only sensible one. To Goldmund's query on the meaning of *sich verwirklichen,* Narziss replies with a reference to the analogy of the artist: "If you have purged the image of a person of all inessential elements and raised it to pure form—then, as an artist, you have realized [*verwirklicht*] this personal image" (V, 288).

Two further motifs which are destined to assume increasing importance in subsequent works appear in the novel: those of service and sacrifice. In the initial conversations, Narziss is clearly conscious of his destiny to serve: "My goal is this: to place myself where I can best serve, where my nature, my characteristics and gifts can find the best soil, the greatest field of effectiveness. . . . Within the limits attainable for me, I intend to serve *Geist* as I understand it, and nothing else" (V, 72). Near the end, Narziss reflects upon the difference in their ways of life. His life is one of "strict service, a continuous sacrifice, an ever renewed striving for clarity and righteousness" (V, 307); but he wonders whether in the eyes of God it is superior to the life of the artist, vagabond, and lover. These twin motifs of service and sacrifice are subsequently explored in *Das Glasperlenspiel*.

V *Style*

Hesse's opinions on this work are somewhat conflicting. On the one hand, he expressed scorn for the host of readers who preferred it to *Steppenwolf* (VII, 494–95), but on the other hand, rereading it after twenty-five years, he found that "nothing in the book summoned him to censure or regret" (VII, 865). The first view may have been provoked by the superficiality of the ordinary reader rather than by inadequacy of the work itself, while the second opinion seems to refute those who see evidence of carelessness,[14] grammatical and stylistic flaws. Deschner has compiled an extensive list of presumed stylistic blemishes of reiteration,[15] including the passage: "Nun *lächelte* die Frau unter seinem erstaunten Blick, *lächelte* sehr freundlich, und langsam begann auch er zu *lächeln*. Auf seinen *lächelnden* Lippen. . . ."[16] Two reservations arise from this evidence: first, the ubiquity of the smile as a major motif in Hesse's work; secondly, the characteristic deliberate cultivation of repetition as a stylistic feature by Hesse. Another passage cited by Deschner is even more reminiscent of this quality analyzed in *Siddhartha:* "Schön war das Leben, schön und flüchtig war das Glück, schön und rasch verwelkte die Jugend."[17] Individual reactions to this style may vary, and some may agree with Deschner that it is no longer possible to write like that in the mid-twentieth century. But it is one side of Hesse's deliberately unrealistic, lyrical approach to the novel.

It seems to me that there is another possible flaw linked with the deliberate use of repetition. The concluding Chorus Mysticus in Goethe's *Faust* reminds us that art depends not on direct exposition but on symbolic suggestion: "Alles Vergängliche ist nur ein Gleichnis" ("Everything transitory is only a parable or metaphor"). Although at the end Goldmund alludes to the mystery that the Great Mother is unwilling to have directly revealed, Hesse elsewhere in the book is both overly explicit and repetitive. The analytical explanations of Narziss in the opening and concluding chapters are open to this criticism. This urge to explain directly and to drive the lesson home is, of course, part of Hesse's didactic tendency.

VI *Pessimism behind the Mediation of Art*

The triadic pattern of development, to which we have become
accustomed in Hesse's works, assumes an unusual aspect in this
novel which presents the parallel development of what are normally successive stages. Goldmund is initially   innocent but
Narziss is already enlightened.

If we, then, focus on Goldmund, we may at first be convinced
that we discern the traditional threefold pattern. In his case, it
is not sex—for this sphere is depicted as part of his instinctive,
natural world—but the murder of Viktor, which clearly marks
his fall from grace, leading to introspection, feelings of guilt,
confession—and ultimately to artistic creation. When we look
for the third stage of illumination in Goldmund's life, we are
faced with a profoundly ambivalent situation. He is successful
in creating monuments which will—for a while—overcome
transience and decay. And he has perceived the mediating relationship of art between mind and matter. But his life is a
failure from many points of view. Boulby perceptively points
to the deeper pessimism underlying this artist novel:

Narziss and Goldmund is . . . superficially a novel of self-realization, but in its essential tenor much more one of tragic resignation.
. . . The two friends are of course not united in any harmonious entity,
but remain utterly separate and different to the very end. Goldmund
may have blended mind and matter in his art, but he has scarcely
done so in his life. . . . [Goldmund's] depersonalization . . . is
unlike that of Harry Haller's Immortals; for it is a sinking back—for
this sensualist who believes in no afterlife—into a formless void. . . .
In *Narziss and Goldmund* the will to be has been sublimated in the
works of art, while life succumbs. . . . Though the book lacks the
stridency of *The Steppenwolf*, it is at bottom an equally painful and
indeed a more pessimistic work. It is a veiled, elusive novel. . . .[18]

CHAPTER 9

Poet and Critic

I   *The Poetry*

HESSE'S reputation will undoubtedly rest on the foundation of his narrative fiction. But the total picture of his life and work would be incomplete without reference to his prodigious productivity both as a lyric poet and as a critic of life and literature. It is the purpose of this chapter to take cognizance of these aspects, before we conclude with an analysis of his *magnum opus, Das Glasperlenspiel.*

Hesse's verse production spans his whole life from 1895 to 1962 and comprises more than a dozen volumes of verse in addition to occasional poems published in journals and implanted in his narrative fiction. By no means all of these items were gathered in the collected works. In his survey of the poetry, Professor Mileck divides the sixty-seven years of production into three periods [1]: the first lasted until the crisis during the First World War in 1916–17 and is characterized by neo-Romantic melancholy and the cult of beauty. We have already given a taste of the *Romantic Songs* in Chapter Two but a fairer example of this first twenty-year span would be the poem "Im Nebel" which appears in numerous anthologies of German verse and which was probably written shortly before its first publication in 1906 [2]:

Seltsam, im Nebel zu wandern!
Einsam ist jeder Busch und Stein,
Kein Baum sieht den andern,
Jeder ist allein.

Voll von Freunden war mir die Welt,
Als noch mein Leben licht war;
Nun, da der Nebel fällt,
Ist keiner mehr sichtbar.

Wahrlich, keiner ist weise,
Der nicht das Dunkel kennt,
Das unentrinnbar und leise
Von allen ihn trennt.

Seltsam, im Nebel zu wandern!
Leben ist Einsamsein.
Kein Mensch kennt den andern,
Jeder ist allein.[3]

It is not necessary to say very much about this poem. It is a good poem of its kind, and one can understand its inclusion in anthologies: its musicality, vowel coloring, its apparent folk-song simplicity with rhymes seeming to evolve of their own (any poet would agree that the attainment of such apparent simplicity and ease involves great art)—all these qualities are there, and yet one cannot escape the feeling that, good as it is, it somehow falls just short of being great. Of course, its epigonal quality is obvious: similar forms, meters, and images had been used for at least a hundred years. But *Epigonentum* is itself a dubious criterion. The "wahrlich" of the third stanza jars, but one may justify it by its function of introducing an expansion of the theme and raising it deliberately into consciousness. Hence it leads us to the didactic trait in Hesse, which tends to make overly explicit what is inherent in the symbols. Similarly, the repetition of the opening line in the last stanza can be seen as a felicitous formal element, and yet it may be linked with the didactic purpose, which repeats in each of the last three lines the explicit meaning.

One can imagine that the theme of this poem would fit into the mid-twentieth century preoccupation of Existentialist writers with the human dilemma of isolation and *Angst*. But the form would be felt as *passé,* for today not a smooth Romantic plaint but a piercing cry would be considered appropriate. This poem, then, symbolizes Hesse's ambivalent position among modern writers, in that he so often voices *avant-garde* problems but clothes them in a conservative, traditional form.

The poem "Blütenzweig" ("Branch in Blossom"), from the volume *Musik des Einsamen, Neue Gedichte* (Heilbronn, 1915), marks the end of the first period and the threshold of a new phase:

> Immer hin und wider
> **Strebt der Blütenzweig im Winde,**
> Immer auf und nieder
> Strebt mein Herz gleich einem Kinde
> Zwischen hellen, dunkeln Tagen,
> Zwischen Wollen und Entsagen.
>
> Bis die Blüten sind verweht
> Und der Zweig in Früchten steht,
> Bis das Herz, der Kindheit satt,
> Seine Ruhe hat
> Und bekennt: voll Lust und nicht vergebens
> War das unruhvolle Spiel des Lebens.[4]

This poem seems to begin with the conventional folk-song strophe, since the opening four lines alternate between three- and four-foot measures and present the rhyme scheme abab. But the stanza is lengthened to six lines with a concluding couplet which establishes not only the rhyme pattern for the second stanza but also its tetrameter rhythm. But the latter is no sooner established when it is interrupted by the shortened line— "Seine Ruhe hat"—which is followed by the lengthened pentameter lines of the concluding couplet. In these verses Hesse is clearly moving away from older, conventional verse forms. The poem was written before *Demian* but it foreshadows the theme of the divided personality and the "light and dark" worlds of Emil Sinclair. Max Schmid[5] sees in this poem a reflection of Hesse's basic dichotomy: the yearning for surrender to nature on the one hand and the reflective consciousness on the other— or in other words, matter and mind. It is a better poem than "Im Nebel," partly because the reflective, didactic element is inherent in the theme, and therefore, legitimately reflected in the form.

In the second period (1916–27), "the plaintive yearning of a nostalgic wanderer becomes the determined quest of a distraught seeker, feeling gives way to thought, self-consciousness to self-awareness and form experiences a corresponding change . . . stanza division, when retained, is very irregular, rime is continued, though quite without pattern, language becomes prosier, its syntax more complex and its vocabulary progressively less romantically evocative, more sober. . . ." [6] This is a good summary, except that to say that the rhyme is "quite without pattern" seems questionable, for sometimes the pattern is there, though less obvious and more subtle, as in the verses of Rilke. Examples of the fluid, changing rhyme patterns can be seen in the *Krisis* poems cited in Chapter Seven. But for the latter verses one cannot claim any intrinsic merit. Their principal interest lies in their confessional nature and in their bearing on *Der Steppenwolf*.

A better example of the lyrical output of this period is the autumnal poem "Vergänglichkeit" ("Transience," 1919):

Vom Baum des Lebens fällt
Mir Blatt um Blatt,
O taumelbunte Welt,
Wie machst du satt,
Wie machst du satt und müd,
Wie machst du trunken!
Was heut noch glüht,
Ist bald versunken.
Bald klirrt der Wind
Ueber mein braunes Grab,
Ueber das kleine Kind
Beugt sich die Mutter herab.
Ihre Augen will ich wiedersehn,
Ihr Blick ist mein Stern,
Alles andre mag gehn und verwehn,
Alles stirbt, alles stirbt gern.
Nur die ewige Mutter bleibt,
Von der wir kamen,
Ihr spielender Finger schreibt
In die flüchtige Luft unsre Namen. [7]

The most conspicuous conventional feature of this poem is its rhyme scheme. The absence of a stanzaic form seems, at first glance, arbitrary since the rhymes suggest that the poem could be divided into four-line stanzas. But a closer perusal indicates subtle changes as the poem develops. The first eight lines offer a regular lilting iambic rhythm in conventional folk-song pattern. With the ninth line, this pattern is abruptly changed by a shift to trochaic and irregular rhythms. Between lines 10 and 11 —exactly midway through the poem—images of death give way to those of birth. Noteworthy in this poem is the absence of an explicit explanation. The images and symbols speak for themselves, referring both to the poet, the reader and everyman. "The eternal mother" thus is able to carry multiple associations: Mother Nature, the Jungian *anima* or instinctive aspect of life, and the poet's mother; all these are to some extent evoked. The imagery is autumnal: falling leaves, a brown grave, bright colors, glowing intoxication. It is, therefore, an autumnal poem, and a better one than those criticized by Deschner.[8]

The third period of Hesse's poetry is characterized by more contemplative and less emotional verse. Outwardly this corresponds to the even tenor of his life with Ninon Ausländer, whom he married in 1931, moving into the Casa Rosa, a house built for him in Montagnola and loaned to him for life by H. C. Bodmer of Zürich.

The mellow mood of his now stable environment is reflected in a longer poem, *Stunden im Garten* (*Hours in the Garden,* 1936) [*G. S.,* V. 323–51] which, both in atmosphere and verse form (hexameters), suggests an affinity with Goethe's *Hermann und Dorothea.* In the garden, Hesse feels himself as part of the whole as he speeds the process of metamorphosis by reducing wood and weeds to ashes and sprinkling them in order to speed new growth in the soil. Like Goethe's protagonists in their idyllic retreat, Hesse reflects on the disturbing events in the outer world:

> Also bescheiden wir uns,
> > und setzen wir möglichst dem Weltlauf
> Auch in drangvoller Zeit
> > jene Ruhe der Seele entgegen,
> Welche die Alten gerühmt und erstrebt,
> > und tun wir das Gute.
> Ohne an Aendrung der Welt gleich zu denken;
> > auch so wird sich's lohnen.[9]

The posthumous poems of Joseph Knecht in *Das Glasper-lenspiel* are good examples of the third period, but these will be considered in the next chapter. Knecht's poems have been praised [10] and pilloried.[11] But the criticism seems to ignore the character of *Gedankenlyrik* (reflective poetry), which has its own norms. Goethe wrote a number of philosophical poems of this kind.

One of the most important poems of this period, to which Hesse referred again and again, is "Besinnung" ("Reflection"), which he "composed on November 20, 1933, in Baden (Switzerland) as an attempt to formulate the few essentials of my faith, of which I am certain."[12]

Göttlich ist und ewig der Geist.
Ihm entgegen, dessen wir Bild und Werkzeug sind,
Führt unser Weg; unsre innerste Sehnsucht ist:
Werden wie Er, leuchten in Seinem Licht.

Aber irden und sterblich sind wir geschaffen,
Träge lastet auf uns Kreaturen die Schwere.
Hold zwar und mütterlich warm umhegt uns Natur,
Säugt uns Erde, bettet uns Wiege und Grab;
Doch befriedet Natur uns nicht,
Ihren Mutterzauber durchstösst
Des unsterblichen Geistes Funke
Väterlich, macht zum Manne das Kind,
Löscht die Unschuld und weckt uns zu Kampf und Gewissen.

So zwischen Mutter und Vater,
So zwischen Leib und Geist
Zögert der Schöpfung gebrechlichstes Kind,
Zitternde Seele Mensch, des Leidens fähig
Wie kein andres Wesen, und fähig des Höchsten:
Gläubiger, hoffender Liebe.

Schwer ist sein Weg, Sünde und Tod seine Speise,
Oft verirrt er ins Finstre, oft wär ihm
Besser, niemals erschaffen zu sein.
Ewig aber strahlt über ihm seine Sehnsucht,
Seine Bestimmung: das Licht, der Geist.
Und wir fühlen: ihn, den Gefährdeten,
Liebt der Ewige mit besonderer Liebe.

> Darum ist uns irrenden Brüdern
> Liebe möglich noch in der Entzweiung,
> Und nicht Richten und Hass,
> Sondern geduldige Liebe,
> Liebendes Dulden führt
> Uns dem heiligen Ziele näher.[1a]

The form is the unrhymed ode in free rhythms which Klop-
stock and Goethe had quickly raised to perfection. The opening
line is strikingly similar to Goethe's "Edel sei der Mensch/
Hilfreich und gut," [14] but the imagery and the thought are typical of Hesse, with the triadic pattern of development toward the
Third Kingdom of *Geist* between the maternal world of nature
and instinct and the awakening of consciousness and moral
responsibility under the aegis of the father-principle. In part the
poem may be regarded as Hesse's answer to the challenge of the
new Nazi regime, with its barbarism and intolerance.

Hesse's last poem, "Knarren eines geknickten Astes" ("Groaning of a Broken Branch"), offers an unusual opportunity to
observe the genetic process. He wrote at least three versions in
the last week of his life, and on the day before his death on
August 9, 1962, he mailed the first and final versions to the
journal *Akzente*. These were reprinted in *Hermann Hesse zum
Gedächtnis*,[15] together with a third, intermediate version. The
first version reads:

> Geknickter Ast, an Splittersträngen
> Noch schaukelnd, ohne Laub noch Rinde,
> Ich sah ihn Jahr um Jahr so hängen,
> Sein Knarren klagt bei jedem Winde.
>
> So knarrt und klagt es in den Knochen
> Von Menschen, die zu lang gelebt,
> Man ist geknickt, noch nicht gebrochen,
> Man knarrt, sobald ein Windhauch bebt.
>
> Ich lausche deinem Liede lange,
> Dem fasrig trocknen, alten Ast,
> Verdrossen klingts und etwas bange,
> Was du gleich mir zu knarren hast.[16]

The final version runs as follows:

Splittrig geknickter Ast,
Hangend schon Jahr um Jahr
Trocken knarrt er im Wind sein Lied,
Ohne Laub, ohne Rinde,
Kahl, fahl, zu langen Lebens,
Zu langen Sterbens müd.
Hart klingt und zäh sein Gesang,
Klingt trotzig, klingt heimlich bang
Noch einen Sommer, noch einen Winter lang.[17]

The difference between the two versions is startling. The first version has twelve lines arranged in traditional stanzas, with regularly alternating rhymes and perhaps too obvious alliteration (knarrt–klagt–Knochen, lausche–Liede–lange). The final poem on the other hand, has a single compact stanza of nine lines containing only two rhymes, the first a tentative one linking the third and sixth lines (Lied–müd), while the second rhyme firmly anchors the last three lines (Gesang–bang–lang). But, more important still, the overt didactic comparison of poet and object has disappeared. The symbol is allowed to speak for itself, and its impact is all the greater.[18] The creative process documented here offers striking proof that Hesse, weakened though he was by leukemia, retained, literally to the last day of his life, his questing, striving character, as he persistently sought a fresher, more adequate and more pregnant form for his last poetic statement.

Any judgment of Hesse as a lyric poet is clouded by the voluminous quantity of his verse. It may even be said that he wrote too much poetry[19] and that only a small part of it will prove of lasting value. But it seems likely that his best poems will continue to find a place in anthologies of the twentieth century.

While it does not throw much light on the quality of his poems, an interesting fact is the enormous number of musical settings they have inspired. The most prominent composition is probably Richard Strauss' *Four Last Songs* for soprano and orchestra. Three of these poems are by Hesse (the fourth is by Eichendorff). The devoted collector of Hessiana, Reinhold Pfau of Stuttgart, compiled in 1966 a vast, unpublished bibliography of such musical settings. It lists 832 published settings of 274 poems by 305 composers. It seems certain that no other poet of the twentieth century has had such an attraction for musicians. But, as Nietzsche points out, of all the arts, music is the lagging *Spätling* (late fruit), so that Handel expressed the best of Luther's soul.[20] Therefore the affinity felt by composers for Hesse's lyrics could be construed as further evidence of the epigonal, conservative quality of this poetry. This would refer, however, mainly to the poems of the first period, for it is these songs which attracted most composers.

II *Literary Critic*

We have already had occasion to observe Hesse as a critic in his Dostoyevsky essays and in his essay on Expressionism (Chapter Five). In addition to the longer critical essays, of which the above are noteworthy examples, Hesse wrote well over a thousand book reviews[21] from the turn of the century until shortly before his death. Despite the modesty with which he regarded his reviews—he claimed that he preferred to say nothing if there was nothing good to be said—many of them in fact reveal a profound critical insight, while others show the way to the future.[22]

At a time when Franz Kafka's greatness was still largely unrecognized Hesse saw both the creative genius and the representative quality of his work:

Later ages will find a game or a serious occupation in recording in retrospect the seismographs of our epoch and in erecting a sequence and hierarchy of those symptoms of unease, upheaval, and despair which the collapse of Christianity has produced in some thinkers and poets. Then one will no longer name Nietzsche and Spengler in one breath . . . one will distinguish more clearly than today those truly involved sufferers from the mere preachers, or even the profiteers, of universal *Angst*. . . . I now believe that the Prague poet Kafka will always be listed among those souls in whom the presentiment of the great upheavals found creative, if painful, expression. . . . There prevails an atmosphere of *Angst* and isolation which is not only unendurable for the philistine but which is hard to breathe for the initiated. . . . Such a clever, such a sensitive and such a responsible human being as Kafka may well, at times, have felt his own writings and thoughts to be destructive and harmful. But we are thankful that they were not destroyed and that these unique, uncanny, admonitory and, at the same time, most lovable works of one mortally stricken have been preserved for us. . . . His phantasy is a burning invocation of reality, an urgent formulation of the religious, existential problem.[23]

It is necessary to bear the date of this review—June 1935—in mind and to remember that the Nazi regime, now more than two years in power, had condemned writers such as Kafka in public book burnings, in order to appreciate Hesse's statement: "With the burning of manuscripts and the surgical excision of symptoms one does not cure illnesses of the age, but one only contributes to evasions and repressions hindering the maturation and brave affirmation of the problems." Thus Hesse combined critical insight into Kafka with some jabs at official attitudes in Nazi Germany.

In his reviews, Hesse ranged widely through world literature, and separate studies have been published of his criticism of English, French, and Russian literature.[24] In 1927 Hesse wrote for Reclam *Eine Bibliothek der Weltliteratur* (*A Library of World Literature*) (VII, 307–43), which is still in print, having been twice expanded in later editions, and which Thomas Mann hailed as an example of supreme humanistic familiarity with the "oldest and most sacred documents of the human mind." [25]

The task of surveying all of Hesse's critical comments on German literature is a much greater project, yet to be undertaken. But for the American reader it may be of interest to examine Hesse's comments on both older and more recent writers in the English language.

In Hesse's introduction to *Gulliver's Travels* we see reflected something of the German author's problematic personality as well as the cultural crisis of our age. Discussing Swift's genius and his struggle with poverty and current social and political problems, Hesse recounts his descent into a state considered by his contemporaries and earlier biographers to be madness:

But it was rather the isolation of a deeply suffering neurotic who was, however, completely unclouded mentally, of a man whose living and thinking had been disastrously isolated and aggravated to a degree of sensitivity no longer endurable. . . . And when finally this Jonathan Swift, out of pure misanthropy, invents a land in which noble horses rule with virtue and reason, when he depicts human beings in this fabled land degenerated into horrible, stinking animals in whom a certain glimmer of reason is only utilized for crime and cynical egoism, . . . how much ardent concern for the future of our species, how much secret, glowing and loving solicitude for humanity, the state, morality and society flare up in this fantastic picture! [26]

The reader will recognize a similar "ardent concern for humanity" and "glowing solicitude for the future" running through Hesse's work from the *Betrachtungen* to *Das Glasperlenspiel*.

Reviewing *The Virgin and the Gypsy*, Hesse compares Hamsun and D. H. Lawrence, subtly delineating the latter's strength and weakness. He finds Hamsun's naive paganism superior to that of Lawrence "which is differentiated, intellectually based and, at times, somewhat neurotically colored. . . . And thus Hamsun's affirmation almost never becomes polemical, while Lawrence goes around almost always armed to the teeth. . . . His paganism lacks Hamsun's innocence."[37]

Hesse criticized Aldous Huxley's *Brave New World* for the utopian unreality of its persons and situations—a weakness which Hesse largely avoided in his own *Glasperlenspiel* through manifold allusions to the Swabian world of the *Tübinger Stift* and its *Klosterschulen*. He then goes on to point out that the novel may be symbolic of Huxley's own tragic situation:

> With acumen and irony a completely mechanized world, in which even human beings are no longer persons but little machines standardized according to the functions expected of them, is depicted. Only two of them are not entirely machines, a superior and an inferior being. They still have remnants of humanity, of soul, of personality, of dream world and passion. Into the picture comes a savage, a complete human being, who inevitably and quickly succumbs in the standardized world of civilization: the last human being. The two half-human beings survive, and one of them may well be the symbol of Huxley's own tragic situation: the figure of the clever, gifted, successful, brilliant *Literat* ["literary man"] who is too much consumed by civilization to be able to become a *Dichter* ["poet," which in German is used of prose and verse writers of first rank], as is his ambition, but who knows very well about the wonder and magic of *Dichtung* [poetry in the widest sense], knows about it more thoroughly perhaps than many a real poet ever knew, for he sees with perfect clarity that *Dichtung* comes from other roots than technology, and that, like religion and genuine scholarship, it is fed on sacrifices and passions which are impossible on the asphalt of a standardized superficial world with its cheap department-store happiness.[38]

Thus we see how Hesse's antipathy to the commercialization and mechanization of life is reflected in his critical reviews as well as in his creative works. His reaction to Jules Verne and

H. G. Wells may, therefore, be anticipated. But it is interesting to observe the strictures he makes in a review of Wells' *In the Year of the Comet:*

All authors like Verne and Wells . . . demonstrate their unphilosophical background and naiveté through bold optimistic predictions, like all utopian writers . . . who only remain interesting as long as they stick to what is purely technical. Beyond that they all engage in fantasies of revolutions and improvements which are supposed to come about through their new machines, powders and motors. The reader becomes weary and thinks: if technology can improve the world, why do we see no results? A flying machine and a projectile to the moon are, to be sure, delightful things, but we cannot easily believe, in the face of universal history, that through them human beings and their relationships can be basically changed. Thus all writers of this harmless species belong to their age and disappear with it, since they are concerned with temporal and incidental things.[29]

The date of this review (1909) is interesting. Hesse lived to see the space age and the American and Russian rivalry in moon rocketry, which may be regarded by many as justifying his pessimistic insight so early in the century.

From various remarks in his reviews one can trace Hesse's attitude to America. From the beginning, he shows a certain ambivalence. On the one hand, he had met pietistic but internationally oriented American missionaries; on the other hand he disliked and distrusted what he regarded as materialistic and technological developments in American civilization tending to produce the mass man. In his early reviews, however, he made exceptions for several Americans in whom he saw evidence of deeper cultural stirrings, notably Walt Whitman and Edgar Allan Poe.[30]

When Hesse comes to Thomas Wolfe, he is, of course, dealing with a kindred spirit—one would like to say "soul brother" —and his review of *Look Homeward, Angel* begins by taking exception to Sinclair Lewis' superficial view of Wolfe's novel and then continues:

Among the many subterranean and nocturnal elements of this work belongs the feeling of life being buried, of the unreality of the real, of the isolation and damnation of every human being, even in the midst of all apparent community. . . . The feeling of being lost, the despair of this poet . . . seems to be the result of a complete lack of faith, religion, authority, and tradition. The hero of this book inherits from his ancestors a strong, healthy, even overflowing sensuality, a flowering fantasy, a powerful hunger for life, even a measure of bonhomie and a considerable amount of talent, but no magic word, no formula of exorcism for the chaos, no name of God, no refuge to prayer, to deep meditation, devotion. . . . One looks forward eagerly [to the next volume] for . . . undoubtedly this hero is the author himself . . . who has become so strongly conscious of himself that there can be only two solutions for him: submersion in the purely sensual—perhaps as an alcoholic like his father—or painful sublimation and a responsible attribution of meaning to life.[31]

Two years later, Hesse reviewed in the same journal Faulkner's *Light in August*, pointing to this author's merits (his concrete, sensuous images) and his shortcomings (unsatisfactory psychology, cinema-like narrative technique).

Writing of J. W. Johnson's *The Autobiography of an Ex-Colored Man,* Hesse shows how forthright he can be in treating current social or political problems:

The American's relationship to the Negro is similar to that of the prosecuting attorney to the criminal, and of the German to the Jew. Johnson's confessions . . . reveal the American Negro in his endearing aspects. No doubt he has other sides, perhaps almost as bad as the white American. As long as the whites have supreme power and treat the Negro like swine, naturally all our sympathies are with the blacks.[32]

Hesse's anti-racist views were also expressed in "Ein Stückchen Theologie" (1932): "In the striving for truth, nothing will be as important and comforting to men as the perception that a unity underlies the division into races, colors, languages, and cultures, that there are different men and minds (*Geister*) but only one humanity, only one *Geist.*" These words were, of course, written not with the American scene in mind but were aimed directly at Germany where Nazi racism was on the threshold of power.

We can measure Hesse's deepened understanding of American life and literature by a review of Salinger's *The Catcher in the Rye* written at the end of 1953. Again his attention is caught by "the highly problematical and threatened existence of a sixteen-year-old American." A masterpiece of conciseness and insight, the review is nevertheless too long to be reproduced in full, but the concluding lines are especially worthy of note:

> Whether one reads this novel as the individual story of a difficult adolescent boy, or whether one reads it as a symbol for a whole land and people, one is led by the author along the beautiful path from alienation to understanding, from repugnance to love. In a problematic world and era, literature can attain nothing higher.[33]

These lines seem to be almost an explicit confession of the course of Hesse's own development of deepened sympathy for American culture. Thus Hesse's criticism throws light from a different angle on themes and attitudes encountered in his creative writing. Prominent among these is the constant striving for deeper insight and awareness.

III *Political and Social Criticism*

It is generally agreed that the novel is the literary genre which most directly reflects political and social criticism, and Hesse's novels—especially *Demian, Der Steppenwolf,* and *Das Glasperlenspiel*—are no exception. The aim of this section, therefore, is simply to draw attention to less well-known examples of his writing in this area, in order to round out the picture of his life and thought.

One of the most astonishing aspects of Hesse's career is the clear-sightedness and consistency of his political views from the beginning to the end of his life. In Chapters Four and Six we have referred to the political essays provoked by the First World War and its aftermath. At a time when Thomas Mann was engaged in a desperate attempt to defend the Prussian and German positions (*Betrachtungen eines Unpolitischen* [*Reflections of an Unpolitical Man*], 1918) Hesse was adamant in his stand against war, against militarism and on behalf of democracy. Although the published correspondence makes the intimate and warm friendship between them perfectly clear, one of the most curious letters of Mann is that of February 8, 1947, where he endeavors, with some casuistry, to defend his record.[34] Two years earlier, he had written to Hesse:

"You were already most articulately resisting the frenzied German pursuit of power, when I was still entangled in romantic-protestant defense of teutomania against revolution and against civilization."[35]

The essays of *Krieg und Frieden* and *Betrachtungen* were followed by Hesse's efforts to assist the development of a sound democratic state through his editing of *Vivos voco* and his associated writings. Becoming disillusioned with the situation in Germany, Hesse gradually dissociated himself from the journal he had helped to found and became a naturalized Swiss in 1923. As we have seen in Chapter Seven, his writing in the mid-1920's showed an increasingly skeptical and critical attitude.

But as the Nazi menace moved closer, Hesse analyzed its character with penetrating insight and foresight. In a diary entry, of July, 1933, he writes of the frightening news from Germany and broods on the acceptance of the Nazi revolution even by good individuals like Otto Hartmann—whose friendship with Hesse dated from the Maulbronn days:

If the [Nazi] "revolution" is not . . . merely of a naive but of a crazy blindness impervious to criticism, hence inwardly false, hostile to organic, life forces, then there is no longer any sense in saying, as Hartmann for instance wrote me: "If this tremendous effort . . . of our nation grows weak and founders, then everything will crash; that must not happen." No, then something will crash for which there need be no regrets; and even if much good blood, much honest German love and idealism suffer this shipwreck and succumb—then it is better to succumb than to be the prop of an organization which is basically evil and satanic. And to me—and I am no politician—the whole attitude of the Third Reich seems evil and satanic. . . .

Hesse goes on to speculate on the naked homage to power which the Nazis share with the Bolsheviks, both having renounced thousand-year-old European and Christian habits, forms, and restraints:

Today there is a break with conventions of humanity, of justice, of international morality. . . . God knows, I do not love this Marxism and its thin rationality, but in order to be comparable with the Soviets, the Third Reich would have to have something more than the swastika and blue eyes.[36]

Two years before the Nazis came to power, Thomas Mann wrote repeatedly to Hesse begging him to accept an invitation to re-enter the Prussian Academy. In December, 1931, Hesse wrote to Mann, attempting to justify his refusal:

In short, I find myself just as remote from the prevailing mentality in Germany as in the years 1914–1918. I am observing processes that I feel to be senseless, and since 1914 and 1918, instead of the tiny step leftward which public opinion has made, I have been driven many miles to the left.[37]

These farsighted political views were not published in the 1930's, and the question arises: Ought Hesse to have engaged in the anti-Nazi polemics which émigré writers—ultimately including Thomas Mann—were to unleash? In defense of Hesse's reticent public position, there are both external and internal arguments. Since 1923 he had been a Swiss citizen, and the Swiss had to be especially cautious in preserving their historic neutral role. Inwardly, Hesse had broken with public life to a large extent, and for his retiring, shy personality a leading role in the market place would have been uncongenial, even unthinkable. Thus he concluded in his 1933 diary:

I feel a kind of obligation to be in the opposition, but I can achieve this in no other way than by neutralizing myself and my work more intensively. I see no way to active opposition, since at bottom I do not believe in socialism. Against the Third Reich, against any state and any exercise of force, I have only the resistance of the individual to the masses, quality against quantity, soul against matter.

Reflecting on his inclination to meditation and withdrawal, he continues: "In short, I am theoretically a saint who loves all humanity, and practically an egoist who never wants to be disturbed. I withdraw from national and social life and half believe that this is somewhat justified by my work which is done in solitude and stillness and which, in the end, belongs to everyone."

Should this work still be available to the German reader in Nazi Germany? Thomas Mann encouraged Hesse to refrain from public statements, which would have led to a prohibition on the sale of his books in the Reich. The spirit of Hesse's writing could not fail to nourish the anti-Hitler forces. But, of course, these lofty arguments are supported by practical considerations. Hesse's income depended on the sale of his books in Germany, for German-speaking Switzerland had a potential market less than 5 per cent of the German in scope. Austria was another outlet but still comparatively minute; and Austria was soon to be swallowed. So during the 1930's and early 1940's Hesse's books were officially regarded as "unerwünscht" (undesirable) but not "verboten" (forbidden), except for those which disappeared for specific reasons, such as *Narziss und Goldmund* (cf. Chapter Eight). As time went on, indirect pressures removed most titles from the list of books in print, for the reprinting could only be done with an allocation of paper, which was more and more consistently refused. Hesse was also bound by loyalty to his publisher, the Jew Samuel Fischer and, when Fischer was forced to liquidate his business, to his successor Peter Suhrkamp.

As it happened, however, Hesse found himself thrust into the center of public controversy as a result of his literary reviews and essays. For nearly two years (1935–36) he served as the German correspondent for the leading Swedish literary journal, *Bonniers Litterära Magasin*. These articles were available only in Swedish translation until the German original from the *Nachlass* was published with commentary by Bernhard Zeller.[38] The attack on Hesse came quickly and was led by Will Vesper, editor of a once prominent anthology of poetry and, ironically, Hesse's predecessor as correspondent for the Stockholm journal, which had had to release him on account of his too rabid Nazi views. In *Die Neue Literatur* of November 1, 1935, Vesper wrote:

In Sweden's . . . leading critical periodical, which is, of course, in Jewish hands, Hermann Hesse . . . a real poet and an Aryan, wrote recently on new German books. . . . He begins . . . with a dithyramb on *Thomas Mann*. . . . Then Hesse declares that "S. Fischer is still the leading publisher in the German book world". . . . The Prague Jewish poet *Kafka* is praised . . . the Jew Alfred *Polgar* . . . the Catholic Gertrud *le Fort*. Then we find the Communist Jew Ernst *Bloch*. Then follows a Viennese Jew Emil *Lucka*. Stefan *Zweig* is mentioned . . . followed by the review of two works of the Jewish scholastic *Maimonides*. . . . Halt, halt, I hear the reader cry. What has Hesse, then, the German poet Hesse, to say about contemporary German literature? This: "[It] . . . shows a tendency to primitive dogmatism and pathetic articles of faith." And this: "A large part of the present 'belletristic' production in Germany bears the stamp of incidental expediency [*Konjunkturen*] and cannot be taken seriously. Adaptations to expediency are always deceptive; the publishers who, for example, turn out all our peasant novels are by no means doing good business . . . but the official criticism proved completely confused and without healthy instincts." Hesse . . . is betraying contemporary German literature to Germany's enemies and to Jewry. . . . The German poet Hermann Hesse is taking over the role of yesterday's Jewish criticism, which was traitorous to the people.[39]

Hesse was understandably angered, although in retrospect it all seems inevitable, for he had written the truth and the truth had hurt. Official representations were made by the president of the Swiss Authors' Association, and Hesse's letter of protest was published in the offending journal, but Vesper persisted in pressing home his charges. Dr. Goebbels' office, however, issued a confidential memorandum ordering an end to these attacks.

Meanwhile Hesse had come under fire from the opposite side, as the militant émigré press—especially the *Pariser Tageblatt*—accused him of making common cause with the Nazi régime and being a collaborator on the Nazi *Frankfurter Zeitung*. The specific charge was, of course, false, but nevertheless the absence of a specific withdrawal of his books from publication and circulation in Germany tended to make his position appear ambivalent.

It is no wonder, then, that Hesse retired from critical writing in 1937 until the end of the Second World War in 1945. In the late 1940's and through the 1950's he published in various places not only literary reviews but comments on political events. The expanded (1946) edition of *Krieg und Frieden* contains half a dozen pieces provoked by the end of the war and the situation in Germany. In a "Letter to Germany" (1946) Hesse analyzes the political attitudes of his correspondents and reflects:

And why had they discovered Hitler only after 1933? Ought they not to have known him at least since the Munich *Putsch* [1923]? Instead of supporting and cherishing the German Republic, the only favorable fruit of the First World War, why had they almost unanimously sabotaged it and voted overwhelmingly for Hindenburg and later for Hitler, under whom, to be sure, it became perilous to be a decent human being? I reminded such correspondents occasionally that the German misery had not even begun with Hitler and that as early as the summer of 1914 the drunken jubilation of the people at Austria's base ultimatum to Serbia really ought to have awakened many. I recounted what Romain Rolland, Stefan Zweig, Frans Masereel, Annette Kolb, and I had had to struggle through and endure in those years. . . . Just as today all my German friends are unanimous in condemnation of Hitler, so they were earlier, on the founding of the German Republic, in condemning militarism, war, and force. . . . "No more wars" was the slogan. But just a few years later, Hitler could venture his Munich *Putsch.* Hence I do not take all too seriously today's unanimity in damning Hitler, and I do not see in it the least guarantee for a political change of attitude nor even for political insight and experience. But I take very, very seriously the change of attitude, the purification and maturity of those individuals for whom in the cruel plight and burning martyrdom of these years there has been opened the Way Within, the Way to the heart of the world, the glimpse into the timeless reality of life. (VII, 447–52)

Just as Hesse had found it difficult to steer his independent course between Nazi and émigré attacks, in the first years after the Second World War he pursued his way between American and Communist camps. In 1946 he was put on a proscribed list through an overly zealous captain of the U.S. Army; and in the 1950's he was accused of being a Communist. He remained, however, as always, independent and critical of mass movements and of force in political life.

His subsequent letters contain most of his comments on these questions. Often such letters were published in various journals, such as the *Neue Zürcher Zeitung, Neue Schweizer Rundschau,* and *Schweizer Monatshefte,* but most, if not all, including most of the latter journal's collection of "political letters,"[40] were included in the expanded edition of *Briefe* (1959) but not in the collected works. And, of course, as a peculiarly intimate exchange of political views the correspondence of Mann and Hesse is unique.

In his message of thanks for the Goethe Prize of the city of Frankfurt in 1946, Hesse included a "moralizing reflection," which reads in part:

I imagine sometimes that Goethe, if he were our contemporary, would agree more or less with my diagnosis of the two major illnesses of the age. In my opinion, there are two mental disorders to which we owe the present condition of humanity: the megalomania of technology and that of nationalism.

In a letter of February, 1955, Hesse declared that he did not believe in any religious dogma and, therefore, not in a God who had created man and thereby made possible the progress from killing with clubs to annihilation with atomic weapons:

From world history I cannot conclude that man is good, noble, peace-loving and selfless; but that among the possibilities open to him, this fine and noble potential, the striving for goodness, peace and beauty, is also present and under fortunate circumstances may reach fruition, this I believe and know for certain. . . . We live surrounded by the apparatus of power and force, often gritting our teeth in indignation . . . we thirst for peace, beauty, freedom for the soaring flights of our souls . . . we feel that we are forbidden to meet force with force. . . . The division of the human world into good and evil is by no means clear-cut; evil lives not only in people of ambition and power but also in us who know ourselves so peace-loving and well-meaning.[41]

In the conclusion of the postscript, written for the Swiss 1946 edition of *Krieg und Frieden,* Hesse speculates about his political clear-sightedness and the factors in his makeup which contributed to it:

Since that first awakening thirty years ago, my response, my reaction vis-à-vis every great political event has always occurred instinctively and completely unsought. My judgments have never vacillated. Now since I am a completely unpolitical person, this reliability in my reaction was always astonishing to me, and I have often reflected upon the sources in which this moral instinct had its origins, I have thought of the pedagogues and educators who, without my having systematically bothered with politics, had so stamped me, that I was always sure of my judgment and possessed a more than average resistance to mass psychoses and mental contagions of every kind. One should admit to what has shaped, stamped, and formed one, and thus after frequent pondering of the question, I must say: there were three strong influences effective throughout my life, which brought about this education in me. There was the Christian and almost completely unnationalistic spirit of my parents' home, there was the reading of the great Chinese, and, last not least, there was the

influence of the only historian to whom I was devoted with confidence, respect, and grateful discipleship: Jacob Burckhardt.

It is astonishing to find Hesse giving two thirds of the credit for
his political sagacity to his reading of the Chinese sages and of
the relatively little-known Basel historian of the nineteenth
century. *Die Morgenlandfahrt* and *Das Glasperlenspiel* will show
these influences at work. however.

CHAPTER 10

Die Morgenlandfahrt *and* Das Glasperlenspiel: *In the Service of* Geist *and* Leben

I Die Morgenlandfahrt

THE importance of this short piece of fiction—published as an *Erzählung* (tale) in 1932—might have warranted a separate chapter in our monograph, but the material is so close to *Das Glasperlenspiel* that one can regard the shorter work as a prolegomenon to the novel, without denying its intrinsic merit.

Die Morgenlandfahrt (*The Journey to the East*) has been justly called Hesse's strangest narrative work. Its esoteric quality and the difficulty of interpretation result from various factors. In the first place, the story purports to be H. H.'s account of his journey to the East with the League, but, as it turns out, the story is not so much a travelogue as it is H. H.'s desperate attempt to compose the story; i.e., *one* of the themes focuses upon the central problem of art: the problem of communicating what is basically a magic, mystical or intuitive insight, using the medium of language, which is normally the vehicle of logic

This reminds us of Hesse's complaint in *Die Nürnberger Reise* of the deficiencies of language as compared with music (cf. Chapter Seven).

Then there are various kinds of deliberate mystifications and hidden allusions. One of these is related to the prototype of the *Bundesroman* (league novel) discussed by Ziolkowski,[1] who demonstrates how at the end of the eighteenth century this sub-literary current entered the mainstream through an influence on the form and content of the Romantic novels—especially some of those which exercised an early fascination on Hesse. Thus *Die Morgenlandfahrt* contains many allusions to mysterious charters, vows of secrecy, passwords, rings, hierarchies, and tribunals.[2] The League of Travelers to the East is composed of figures related to Haller's "Immortals," forming a body reminiscent of Plato's governing philosophers. Early in the text, this affinity is tentatively suggested by "a few advances made into the realm of a future *Psychokratie*" ("rule of soul or mind"—which the American translator, unfortunately, rendered by "psychiatry"!).[3]

Other kinds of mystification seem to have been part of Hesse's ironic, playful approach, e.g., the ciphers in the archives referring to himself: "Chattorum res. gest. XC. civ. Calv. infid. 49" which is only partly revealed by translating: "Hesse's deeds and works XC, citizen of Calw who became unfaithful in 49." The numbers still remain enigmatic, although Ziolkowski speculates that the second figure might indicate apostasy to the Order in 1926, when Hesse was forty-nine years old.[4]

To this category belong the playful references to actual persons, places, and events. Max and Tilli (Wassmer) were the couple who owned Schloss Bremgarten near Berne and frequently entertained Hesse and his friends, among whom were, of course, his patron Hans C. Bodmer, whose house in Zürich was called "Zur Arche"; and this reference is compounded by an encapsulated allusion to his eighteenth-century namesake J. J. Bodmer, the composer of an epic on Noah (VI, 24). Other actual persons present at Bremgarten include Longus (the psychoanalyst and scholar of ancient religions Dr. J. B. Lang), Louis (Moilliet), the Swiss painter, Othmar (Schoeck), the Swiss who composed music for many of Hesse's poems, and Ninon "the foreigner" (*die Ausländerin*, a playful allusion to Hesse's wife, whose maiden name was Ausländer).

But the travelers to the East include not only actually living persons but real deceased persons ranging from Lao Tse, Zoroaster, Plato, Xenophon, Pythagoras, Albertus Magnus, and Novalis to Baudelaire and Hugo Wolf. Furthermore, these characters are freely interspersed among others from the world of fiction: Don Quixote, Tristram Shandy, Parzival, Witiko, and Hesse's own creations, Klingsor, Siddhartha, Vasudeva, Goldmund, and Pablo, who is ironically disguised as Mozart! Although the theme of H. H.'s desperate and inadequate attempt to narrate the journey recurs constantly, we do nevertheless obtain glimpses of the nature of this quest:

The narration is further complicated by the fact that we wandered not only through space but, in just the same way, also through time. We traveled to the East, but we also traveled into the Middle Ages or into the Golden Age; we roamed through Italy or Switzerland; we spent the night, however, at times in the tenth century and sojourned with patriarchs or elves. (VI, 23)

It thus becomes clear that, in one sense, the journey beyond time and space leads into the realm of art, where one can roam freely through the whole body of culture. The past and the present, the real and the fictional are united in common allegiance to the Order. On his first initiation, H. H. learns that each member must have his unique individual mission in the common pilgrimage to the East. Each in his separate way contributes to the common goal. The members resemble Haller's Immortals but also point forward to the Castalians of *Das Glasperlenspiel*.

The East represents not merely those oriental sages and figures among the members but symbolizes the universality of *Geist*, embracing all who have penetrated behind apparent reality, beyond differentiation and individuation to oneness. All the figures, whether real or imagined, form part of the eternal *Geist*. This term means more than "mind" or "spirit" and here extends to the sum of achievements of the human mind throughout the ages.

The allusions, more or less thinly disguised, to actual persons and places make this work, in one sense, a *roman à clef*—a characteristic which it shares with *Das Glasperlenspiel*. But in neither work does this aspect dominate. It is not necessary to have the clues in order to appreciate their meaning on their more important levels of interpretation.

Das Glasperlenspiel

Die Morgenlandfahrt is a *roman à clef* in another sense, which can be inferred by the reader who has only a modest acquaintance with the author's life and work. This aspect is described by Ziolkowski in the phrase "symbolic autobiography." [5] In his words, "the geographical movement . . . takes us from South Germany and Swabia through Switzerland to Montagnola (called *Montags-Dorf* in the text)—the course of Hesse's own life." More important, however, is the inner spiritual biography. This can be conceived again in terms of the triadic pattern which Hesse claimed as a prime article of his faith in *Ein Stückchen Theologie*, published in the same year. H. H. has joined the League to journey to the East under the initial enthusiasm of innocence, suggested by the literary references to Romantic works in the early chapters, but more expressly symbolized by the object of his individual quest on admittance to the Order: the Princess Fatme, an innocent fairy-tale figure fascinating to the Romantically inclined youth. Near the end he reflects:

I was overwhelmed with the realization of the sweet magic which had enfolded me when I began my pilgrimage to the East, and when I remembered how the pilgrimage had been wrecked by malicious and basically unknown obstacles, how the magic had more and more evaporated, and what desolation, soberness, and cold despair had since been my breath, my bread, my drink. . . . Alas, today I felt the image of the Arabian princess would no longer suffice to arm me against the upper and under worlds and to make me a knight and crusader; today a different, stronger magic would be required. But how sweet, how innocent, how sacred that dream had been in search of which I had set forth in my youth, which had made me a reader of fairy tales and made me a musician and novitiate and had led me to Morbio Inferiore!

In *Ein Stückchen Theologie,* Hesse summarizes the triadic pattern: "The Way leads out of innocence into guilt, out of guilt into despair, from despair either to destruction or to redemption: that is to say, not back beyond morality and civilization into the childhood paradise, but beyond it into the ability to live by virtue of one's faith" (VII, 391). The parallel with the fictional H. H. is clear: his incurring of guilt on losing faith and abandoning the pilgrimage to the East, and his ensuing despair which threatened destruction, followed by his recovery of faith on a higher level and his re-admittance under different auspices. Leo clarifies this when he passes sentence:

Through his testing Brother H. has been led into despair, and despair is the result of every serious attempt to comprehend and justify human life. Despair is the result of every serious attempt to withstand life with virtue, with justice and reason, and to fulfill its demands. On one side of despair live the children, on the other the awakened. The accused H. is no longer a child and not yet quite awakened. He is still in the midst of despair. He will stride beyond it and thereby enter his second novitiate. (VI, 68)

It is clear, then, that Boulby is right in claiming that a purely esthetic interpretation of the work is inadequate.* On one level, the work deals with art and the artist and the latter's desperate attempt to communicate the inner mystery. But on another plane, it presents the existential problem of Everyman; and it does so in terms that allude to twentieth-century thought: do I exist? how do I know that I exist? Only by doing, by creating can I prove that I exist. At the end of Chapter Three, H. H. "perceives every day more clearly" that his efforts to write this book stem not from a noble cause, for which sacrifice was worthwhile, but simply from "the striving to save my life, by giving it new meaning."

So far we have said little about Leo the Servant, whose role is obviously central to the book. It was his mysterious disappearance in the gorge of Morbio Inferiore which led to the disbandment of the pilgrims and the loss of faith by H. H. and his companions. Even in the capacity of servant, Leo had held the group together, and the strength of his personality had far transcended his humble role. When he is revealed as the Head of the Order in the hall of judgment, the humbler qualities remain a part of him. Clothed in the ornate robes of office he stepped down from the throne, shook the hand of H. H., "looked me in the eyes, smiled his devout bishop's smile, and was the last to leave the chamber" (VI, 71). The smile reminds us of Siddhartha, Vasudeva, and Mozart in earlier works, but the attendant circumstances have changed. Here the smile is attached to one in whom the polar opposites of the highest and the lowest, of supreme authority and humblest service are unified and united. In this respect, he is the prototype of Joseph Knecht and a more interesting figure than H. H.

But is Leo distinct from H. H.? We must consider the enigmatic ending of the tale, when H. H., given the authority to consult the archives on any subject, finally pulls out the drawer marked *Chattorum res gestae* and finds only a double statuette of two figures molded back to back in a transparent substance. One face belongs to him, while the other represents Leo. Observing more closely, he becomes aware of an internal process,

something like a very slow, gentle, but uninterrupted flowing or melting; and in fact it was flowing or running out of my image over into Leo's, and I recognized that my image was engaged in giving itself to Leo, in streaming into him, nourishing and strengthening him. In time, so it seemed, all substance would run out of the one image into the other and only a single one would remain: Leo. He had to wax, I had to wane. (VI, 75–76)

This ending recalls Emil Sinclair's absorption of Demian, but again the circumstances and the meaning have changed. The enigmatic words have been interpreted, quite properly, with reference to the esthetic theme. Some variations are possible even within these limits, but in the main the message seems to point to the importance of the fictional figure over that of his creator. This point had been alluded to several times earlier in the story: "But even if these artists, or some of them, were very lively and charming characters, the figures invented by them were, without exception, much more lively, more beautiful, happier and, to a certain extent, more correct and more real than the creators and poets themselves" (VI, 27).

This obviously refers to the heightened and continued vitality of the great figures who form part of our living past in literature and art. But it points also to a change in Hesse's esthetic which tends now to de-emphasize the idiosyncratic personal element and enhance the supra-personal or objective aspect of art. It also points forward to the Castalian creed in *Das Glasperlenspiel*, which eschews egocentricity and subordinates the individual to the higher ideals of the Order and the immortal *Geist* it represents.

On the other hand, since the esthetic interpretation is only one of several, the fusion of H. H. into Leo may symbolize the growth of the polar qualities of service and authority or, more explicitly, of the awareness that the role of *Geist* should be service, and that through service and sacrifice authority and effectiveness are achieved. This, too, points forward to the career of Joseph Knecht, whose name, of course, means "servant" in

German. On a more esoteric or philosophical level, one can see in this symbolism a hint of the theme of the oneness of humanity, transcending individual differences of race or creed.

Despite the frustrations of the creative artist and the existential despair of Everyman, the message is more optimistic than ever before in Hesse. The Order—and the ideals and esthetic forms and values which it cherishes—does exist, and the humble and despairing postulant is accepted and welcomed into the Order of the elect. We are thus prepared for the even more positive treatment of the Castalian Order in *Das Glasperlenspiel*.

II Das Glasperlenspiel:
Genesis, Structure, and Perspectives

Das Glasperlenspiel is a complex work full of dichotomies—some of them true or intended polarities—and ambiguities, not all of which are resolved. No other work of Hesse has· stimulated so much discussion, most of it eulogistic but some quite critical.[7] We must remember that we are dealing with a work of literature, and not with a system, be it of philosophy, esthetics, or religion. Hesse once complained in a letter to a doctoral candidate that the latter was attempting what all the books, essays, and dissertations on him attempted, namely to "freeze the fluctuating life of a poet and his work in conceptual, dogmatic categories. . . . And then what does *Weltanschauung* mean? You seem to imply by it that a human being must necessarily have a definite philosophy of life throughout his life or at least through certain periods thereof. But we poets are not such poor devils, and I hope most other people are not."[8] The passage explicitly points to Hesse's lifelong preoccupation with metamorphosis and constant change in perspective and development. Nevertheless, the critic is obliged, to a certain extent, to attempt the impossible: to fix and logically analyze the many questions of substance raised by the work. To what extent are the Castalian Order and the Glass-Bead-Game chiliastic in conception and intent? What is the meaning of Knecht's defection and of his death? What is the nature of the Game and what does it represent? What is the role of the individual? If service and sacrifice, to what? How are we to weigh the different perspectives of the Castalian narrator, of the Legend, of Knecht's conversations and of his poems and imaginary autobiographies?

Das Glasperlenspiel

Why are the Castalians without a historical sense? What are the roles of such problematical characters as the Chinese Brother, Tegularius, and the "shadow," Bertram—to say nothing of the less problematical figures, such as Pater Jacobus and the Music Master? Is there an underlying Hegelian dialectic? What other influences may be imbedded in the fabric of Hesse's thought? Some of these problems will be explored in this and the following sections, and the discussion of music (section V) will provide a key to the major themes.

A study of the genesis of *Das Glasperlenspiel* will help us in the examination of certain questions and will bring into sharper focus others which may be unanswerable. We know that Hesse began to work on this project in 1930 or 1931, and that therefore it took root simultaneously with *Die Morgenlandfahrt*, whose League of Pilgrims to the East represents the prototype of the Castalian Order.

The dates of first publication of certain parts of this novel are of interest. The first two parts to appear were the introductory chapter and one of the last sections, the first of the appended "Lives," namely "Der Regenmacher," in *Die Neue Rundschau* in 1934. The same journal published "Der Beichtvater" ("The Father Confessor") and "Indischer Lebenslauf" ("Indian Life") in 1936 and 1937. Seven further chapters appeared, some in the same periodical, and others in *Corona,* at various dates between 1938 and 1942. In some instances, passages directly hostile to the Nazi regime were deleted.' Of Knecht's thirteen poems, seven appeared in *Corona* (1935), and the remaining six in various journals between 1936 and 1942. The most important poem, "Stufen," was the last to be published. It is a curious fact that the poem which seems to conjure up a picture of annihilation and destruction in the war was actually a prophetic vision: "Der letzte Glasperlenspieler" (*National-Zeitung,* Basel, 1937).

The critical period in the genesis of the novel, however, lies in the years prior to 1934. From the literary remains, deposited in the Schiller-Nationalmuseum, it is now possible to throw light on some of the problems. But we must first consider the now published letter of Hesse to Rudolf Pannwitz, of January, 1955, in which Hesse declared that the initial impulse for writing had been the idea of reincarnation as a "form of expression of what is constant within transience, of the continuity of tradi-

tion and of the life of the spirit and intellect." [10] Hesse went on
to state that, years before he began to write the novel, he had
had a vision of a "transcendental biography . . . of a being who
in several incarnations shared the experience of the great epochs
of human history." Carried over from this idea were the three
appended "Lives"—and the suppressed but now published
fourth—and also certain aspects of Knecht's Castalian career.
This intention seems confirmed by a fragmentary note in the
Nachlass which must date from the earliest period of composition, for the hero is as yet unnamed and is viewed as the narrator: "Reincarnation as the present X who narrates the story. The
legend of X . . . wills not (?.) to be born again."

Actually, in the three constituent "autobiographies" there is
little trace of the "experience of great epochs of history," for
the first involves a prehistorical matriarchal society, and the second deals with religious recluses. The "Indian Life," however,
does retain the motifs both of metempsychosis and of dynasties,
wars, and destruction (for these are the raw materials of history), but as illusions of *Samsara*. The fourth, the early eighteenth-century *Lebenslauf*, provides for Knecht an incarnation
in the great age of Western music.

In his letter to Pannwitz, Hesse described how the work had
been germinating in his mind in changing shapes, "now solemn,
now playful," as evil emanations began to arise from the Nazis
in Germany, before and after their accession to power. Faced
by these potential perils, Hesse states, he fell back upon the
recourse open to artists, i.e., production. He took up this projected work "in order to build a spiritual realm in which I
could live and breathe in defiance of all the poison in the
world," and secondly, "in order to strengthen my friends in
Germany in perseverance and resistance." In depicting the
"realm of the intellect and soul as extant and invincible," and
in banishing "the evil present into a past that had been overcome," Hesse claims to have created his utopia of Castalia
unconsciously.

Documents in the *Nachlass*, however, reveal the evolution of
the concept of the Glass-Bead-Game, and with it of the Castalian Order, from quite banal beginnings, inextricably bound up
with the sharpest criticism of the political conditions in Germany. [11] In a preliminary version of the introductory chapter of
the novel, we are told that people in the "Feuilleton Age" could

hardly cross the street without being roared at or kicked by armed men. Two imaginary books published in 1950 (the passage was written in 1931) are discussed by Hesse. *The War Guilt Lie* by Professor Lankhaar "proves" the innocence of the German "Volk," the Kaiser, the General Staff, and the Foreign Office, forty years after everyone else had forgotten about the war of 1914–1918. The second book, *The Green Blood,* reveals Hesse's sarcasm even more directly, for this "green blood," like a holy stigma, was held to be the mystical mark of a select few, genuine *Führer* natures, who had resulted from at least thirty generations of pure Germanic race. The origin of the "bead-game" in this early version lies in the familiar German card game of *Dichterquartett,* and the beads were first used as a kind of abacus to record points won—blue for poets, red for musicians, etc.

In an unpublished diary of July, 1933—six months after the rise of the Nazis to power—Hesse recounts how, reading the preliminary version of the introductory chapter, written nearly two years earlier, he was startled to perceive the pattern of events in Germany predicted so accurately that it sounded almost like a parody. He concluded that it was too *zeitgebunden* (topical) and would have to be rewritten. And so it was, with startling changes,[12] most of which tend toward "alienation" and universalization, so that most of the specific or thinly veiled references to Germany and Hitler disappeared from the text. Instead of a political novel with a sharp indictment of things German, we have a work of cultural and social criticism, focused upon those aspects of Western civilization that seemed to Hesse decadent or problematical; and we have, on the other hand, the polar or counter-forces of Castalia, representing *Geist* or the eternally valid spiritual and intellectual legacy of the past, which continues into the present and the future. But the Castalian historian, viewing the twentieth century, adopts the attitude already evinced by Hesse in *Blick ins Chaos,* namely that Western man and his works had to continue downhill to a low point of chaos before a new birth could take place: "There had first to take place a demolition of what was *passé* and a certain realignment of the world and of morality, before the civilized world of culture became capable of a real self-critique and of a new order" (VI, 95).

In the novel's final form, the narrator views our "warlike"

age almost as from another planet, as the serene Castalians look back from a period some four centuries hence. The historian concludes that our "warlike" or "feuilleton" age had been characterized by excessive indiscipline, flippancy, and irresponsibility of intellectual life, by a "horrendous devaluation of language" (VI. 93). One of the polarity motifs is revealed here (with a suggestion of Hegelian dialectic), for it was just these mass excesses which "conjured up in the smallest circles that antithetical movement" (VI, 93) of austerity and restraint, which produced Castalia and the Glass-Bead-Game.

It has been contended by Ziolkowski that Hesse's original intention was purely utopian, and that the author's attitude changed as the work progressed, leaving unresolved discrepancies.[13] The earliest sketches in the *Nachlass* reveal, however, that from the beginning Hesse regarded Castalia and the Game as subject to the problematical forces of history, forces which would involve vicissitudes and a "defection" on the part of Knecht:

Knecht prepares and executes the great yearly game at the height of his powers. . . . After finishing the game, he resigns his office as *magister* . . . he wants to go into the world, he is unwilling to serve any longer here where all is so perfect, but outside among strangers. . . . He will attempt to radiate there something of what he brings from here: readiness to serve. . . . Here, among intellectuals, that is easy. Out there, in the open market of passions, it is more difficult.[14]

Another note observes that "the deprived, uncultured masses destroy everything (with justification) for the bead-players are in their eyes ridiculous and repugnant." [15] The parenthetical remark, "with justification," clearly indicates the anti-utopian perspective of this early notation.

These early working papers, almost certainly dating from 1930–31, also emphasize the themes of sacrifice and service, as the longer quotation above indicates. The utopian question is not as simply resolved, however, for Castalia is simultaneously utopian and anti-utopian. It is utopian in its chiliastic projection and in its rarefied intellectual and esthetic idealism, but is shown to be subject to the ebb and flow of history and prone to hubris, harboring disdain for "life," as we see in arch-Castalians such as Tegularius. In one sense, the Castalian Order represents exactly what the League represented in *Die Morgenlandfahrt,* namely, all those artists and thinkers, both past and present, who, whether alone or in concert, preserve and pass on the cultural heritage. In a letter of 1944, Hesse wrote:

> The utopian element, that is the transposition into the future, is, of course, only an expedient. In reality, Castalia, Order, meditative scholarliness, etc. is neither a futuristic dream nor a postulate, but an eternal, platonic idea which has already been realized on earth in various degrees: (VII, 641)

The introductory chapter stands apart as a separate historical background to Joseph Knecht's "biography." Looking back from the year 2400 A.D., the chronicler perceives that European intellectual life since the end of the Middle Ages has had two main tendencies, "the liberation of thought and belief from all authoritative influence . . . and—on the other hand—the secret but passionate search for legitimization of this freedom, on the basis of a new adequate authority inherent in the mind itself" (VI, 88). The parodied chronicle style heightens the ironical criticism, since human life in the twentieth century seems almost incredible to the serene Castalian, who records how the masses sought release from the *Angst* produced by political, economic, and moral upheavals and by terrible wars and civil strife. Some retreated to crossword puzzles, others sought diversion in reading or listening to the proliferation of excess verbiage, in feuilletons or public lectures, on such topics as "Friedrich Nietzsche and Female Fashions in the Year 1870," "The Favorite Dishes of the Composer Rossini," or "The Role of the Lap Dog in the Life of Great Courtesans." This flood of words bore "the stamp of quick, irresponsibly manufactured mass production" (VI, 91).

Behind this sociological analysis lie two probable influences. Huizinga's *Homo Ludens* was almost certainly influential in forming Hesse's concept of "play" as the highest manifestation of culture. The same work may also illustrate the nature of Hesse's criticism of our age, for Huizinga wrote of "puerilism" in our cultural life as resulting from the "entry of half-educated masses into intellectual communication, the relaxation of ethical standards, and the extreme communicability which technology and organization have bestowed on society."[16] This also reflects *The Revolt of the Masses* of Ortega y Gasset, whose influence on his thinking Hesse readily conceded.[17] The Castalian chronicler speaks of a "flood of eager scribbling on every daily event" and of the growing awareness—present since Nietzsche—"that the late age, the twilight, of our culture had begun." The symptoms include "the dreary mechanization of life, the low ebb of morality, the lack of faith of whole nations, the charlatanism of the arts. Corruption entered the schools, journals, universities . . . and raged as uncontrolled, dilettantish overproduction in all the arts" (VI, 94). The antithetical movement, which later developed into Castalia, began at this low point of cultural life, among a few isolated individuals devoted to mathematics and music.

The device of a fictitious narrator writing a "biography" or editing "posthumous papers" was used by Hesse throughout his career, beginning with *Hermann Lauscher;* and we saw in *Der Steppenwolf* how this device contributed to the creation of multiple perspectives. The same effect is achieved in *Das Glasperlenspiel,* where the poetic vitality of Joseph Knecht's own "writings" contrasts with the ironic, pedantic, playful, and equivocating chronicle style of the Castalian narrator. The latter shows a marked affinity with Serenus Zeitblom in *Doktor Faustus,* as Thomas Mann observes in his diary: "This prose [Hesse's] is as close to me as if it were a piece of myself. . . . I was almost frightened at its affinity with what was so urgently preoccupying me. The same idea of a feigned biography—with the elements of parody which this form brings with it." [18]

Thomas Mann wrote to Hesse of his delight, especially in the "serious playfulness" (*ernste Verspieltheit*), pointing out that Hesse's novel was itself a kind of Glass-Bead-Game—a "playing with all the contents and values of our culture" at a level on which the "capacity of universality is reached, hovering above the faculties." Readers and critics who treat *Das Glasperlenspiel* as if it were a closed philosophical system should heed Mann's next statement: "This transcendence, of course, involves irony, which makes the solemn, reflective whole nevertheless into a subtle joke, full of cunning, and is the well-spring of its humor as parody of the biographical and grave academic façade. People will not dare to laugh, and you will be secretly vexed at their stiff, earnest respect. I know that sort of thing." [19]

Das Glasperlenspiel

This style may be considered characteristic of *Alterswerke,* but Hesse's novel differs from Mann's in combining this feature with attributes of a more direct, youthful, "poetic" style. It must be admitted that Hesse has not always confined the two styles to the appropriate sections of the work,[20] but the problem was difficult, since the more direct, "poetic" style is not confined to the poems and "lives" of Knecht and his "legend," but occurs throughout in frequent conversations and quotations.

A little more than half of the novel traces the development of Knecht from boyhood to his elevation as *magister ludi,* his defection and death. This part has the form of a *Bildungsroman,* and the reader who approaches it as such may be puzzled at the long introduction and the several hundred pages of apparent appendices. But these are not gratuitous accretions, for they retrospectively illuminate the meaning of Knecht's life and death and provide the basis for understanding the role of Castalia. This structure is shared, to some extent, by Boris Pasternak's *Doctor Zhivago,* where the hero's posthumous poems also throw light on a novel of individual development, which is, however, far more diffuse and uncontrolled than Hesse's work.[21] In discussing the features shared by Goethe's *Wilhelm Meisters Wanderjahre* and *Das Glasperlenspiel*—especially those characteristic of *Alterswerke*—Thomas Mann declared that Hesse's novel was a "rounded-off masterpiece complete in itself," whereas *Die Wanderjahre* seemed a "hoch-müde, würdevoll sklerotisches Sammelsurium."[22] Despite this claim to superiority over both *Die Wanderjahre* and *Doctor Zhivago* in unity and tightness of organization, it cannot be maintained that *Das Glasperlenspiel* is entirely free of whimsicalities, gratuitous reflections, and unresolved ambiguities, some of which have been pointed out by Siegfried Unseld.[23]

Das Glasperlenspiel is a *Bildungsroman* and yet far exceeds the limits of this genre. It is a utopian novel and yet at the same time strongly anti-utopian. It is a novel of social, cultural, and political criticism, but only in part so; it is a novel permeated by music, both directly and indirectly, and is therefore a peculiar kind of *Künstlerroman* in a milieu where *Kunst,* in the sense of real creativity, is eschewed or forbidden; and it is a biographical and autobiographical novel which is projected both ways: into a remote future depicted with playful whimsicality, but also into the familiar past—portrayed with even more playful whimsicality. For the whole Castalian Order, with its preparatory and élite schools, resembles a glorified, world-embracing *Tübinger Stift*,²⁴ similar to that into which Hesse and Hans Giebenrath entered, after they had passed the entrance examination in Stuttgart. Young Knecht's first confrontation with the Music Master is a purified re-enactment of this critical examination and the first "awakening," just as Knecht's "defection" is the manifestation of a new "awakening," which repeats, on a more exalted plane, the flight of Hesse and of Hermann Heilner from Maulbronn. Unlike most utopian novels, this world of the future is devoid of technological gadgetry and in many respects is closer to the 1890's than it is to our world. The English translator and many critics have failed to preserve the deliberate ambiguity of words like *Wagen*, which may equally denote a horse-drawn carriage or a motor car. The political relationships reflect bourgeois-democratic party struggles. Either Marx has left no mark on history or more likely, we are actually transposed backwards in time to a pre-socialist era. The novel is thus also a *roman à clef*, for, as in *Die Morgenlandfahrt*, there are many open or veiled references to real and fictional persons and places in Hesse's life.

Das Glasperlenspiel is a kind of *Überroman* (super-novel), both in the narrower connotation of Curtius' distinction between *Überroman*²⁵ (in the sense of Freedman's lyrical novel) and *Aktionsroman*, and in a wider syncretistic sense. It marks Hesse's furthest step towards *Essayismus* in the novel, a trend carried furthest, among Hesse's contemporaries, by Robert Musil, Ernst Jünger, and Hermann Kasack.²⁶ But Hesse and Thomas Mann, for all their formal experimentation, are both simultaneously continuers of tradition and innovators. In *Das Glasperlenspiel*, form and content are closely connected. It seems peculiarly appropriate that this novel should combine hybrid forms of the past and present—and possibly of the future—when one of its major themes revolves around the continuity and projection into the future of our cultural heritage. In style and perspective the novel exemplifies the principle of polarity. We shall see this principle at work in the following section.

III   *Portraits and Polarities in* Das Glasperlenspiel

As we have observed, *Das Glasperlenspiel* is, to a minor degree, a *roman à clef*. Thomas Mann was quick to recognize himself in the *magister ludi*, Thomas von der Trave, and was amused at Hesse's portrayal of his ethical and esthetic nature, for the Glass-Bead-Game stands for art and especially music and literature, just as the problems of music in *Doktor Faustus* symbolize the novelist's dilemmas. Thomas von der Trave was "a hard worker . . . in matters pertaining to the Game, of guarded and ascetic strictness. . . . His brilliantly constructed, formally unsurpassable Games revealed to the connoisseur a close intimacy with the background problems of the realm of the Game" (VI, 219).

Later we are told that two types of Game were discerned, the "formal" and the "psychological" (VI, 84), and we learn that both Knecht and Tegularius were among the devotees of the latter, but that Knecht preferred to use the term "pedagogical" rather than "psychological." This points to a didactic tendency in Hesse's writing, which developed to its furthest point in this last novel. Not only are there "lessons" to be inferred from the basic themes of the work and from the criticism of our age, but the Castalian Order is, in part, a teaching order (as is the Benedictine), and Knecht is increasingly drawn to teaching. The younger the pupils, the greater his pedagogical satisfaction.

The inclusion of Tegularius among the "psychological" players conflicts, however, with his character as developed in the book, for he represents the formalist, the arch-Castalian, who is concerned with esthetic form alone and is not interested in "life" or history. Why did Hesse obscure his characterization here? Probably because Fritz Tegularius is a portrait of Friedrich Nietzsche, whose work is noted for its psychological probing. Since the portrait is a sympathetic one, it is fair to assume that Hesse is paying tribute to an earlier influence of Nietzsche in his thinking, as does Thomas Mann in *Doktor Faustus*.

Hesse's characterization, apart from Knecht, tends to be flat, lacking the fullness and roundness which would fully engage our sympathy and attention. In part this is so because, while we

view Knecht from various perspectives, the others are revealed
on one plane only. But this lack of plasticity in the other characters also results from the fact that all of them exist only in relation to Knecht, and that each is a representation of one facet
of the hero. Knecht is composed of multiple, polar aspects,
which are reflected in those around him. Thus the other characters tend to fall into polarized categories. This seems to be the
first principle of characterization in the book, for Hesse's attention is focused on two main things: Castalia, of which the
Glass-Bead-Game is the *summum bonum,* and the exemplary
figure of Joseph Knecht. The second principle is the playful,
sometimes ironic portrayal of real persons (including himself)
of the past and present, as in *Die Morgenlandfahrt.* Sometimes
the two principles are united, as in Tegularius, who represents
a rarefied Castalian formalism and is also a portrait of
Nietzsche.

When we think of the influences which mold Knecht's character and which become part of him, each tends to become iden-
tified primarily with one figure. The most important influence
is that of music, which, together with the exemplary figure of
the *Altmusikmeister,* will form the subject of section five of
this chapter. Tegularius represents the attraction for Knecht of
the Castalian contemplative life which eschews history. The
opposite tendency toward history, together with a sense of
involvement in it, is reflected in Pater Jacobus. The Chinese
Brother seems to represent the wisdom of the East and the spirit
of meditation (the *vita contemplativa*), but as we shall see
shortly, there may be a latent ironical interpretation of this
enigmatic outsider in the bamboo grove. Plinio Designori
awakens in Knecht his longing for the opposite pole, the active
life. The major theme of service and sacrifice is suggested by
more than one character: by the music master's devotion to
music *and* to his pupils; by Designori's inherited *noblesse
oblige;* and possibly in the strange figure of the "shadow,"
Bertram, whose fate seems so cruel and so anti-Castalian to
Boulby. Boulby refers to Jung's concept of the "shadow" as a
representation of the personal unconscious: "The meaning,
then, at least in part, is that all masters must have their
'shadow' and that in fact the 'shadow' can never come to be the
master." " But it is also possible that Bertram's stoically accepted
fate prefigures Knecht's acceptance of the role of sacrificial

victim. Bertram's sacrifice, however, is made in the service of the hierarchy,[28] whereas Knecht's is intended to be made in a higher synthesis of *Geist* and *Leben*.

Pater Jacobus is a figure of major importance. He is a Roman Catholic and a Benedictine. Through him we meet another kind of institution and an order which is, in many respects, a polar opposite of Castalia. In fact, Knecht is given the diplomatic mission to attempt to bridge the dichotomy between these disparate realms. Christianity is based on the sacrifice of Christ. The Benedictines are monks, but their *raison d'être* lies in their healing mission and in service to suffering humanity, while the Castalians serve only *Geist*. As a portrait of the historian Jacob Burckhardt, the pater provides a similar message. Hesse himself acknowledged the influence of Burckhardt's investigations into the role of the individual in historical crises and into the interrelations of the three *Potenzen*, state, religion, and culture.[29] The importance of Jacobus for Knecht's development is overwhelming, since his views on the state and religion form "the basis for Knecht's defection from Castalia, for they summarize, in brief, his rejection of the aesthetic abstraction of the Glass Bead Game and his realization that Castalia, as an institution, can claim no eternal validity." [30]

The full significance of the *Altmusikmeister* will be dealt with in section five, but we may, at this point, briefly speculate on his identity. Hesse himself serves as a possible model, especially in his cultivation of silence during his last years.[31] Other suggested models are Goethe[32] and the eighteenth-century Swabian theologian Friedrich Christoph Oetinger (1702–82).[33] The most recently suggested prototype, however, is Hesse's grandfather Hermann Gundert.[34] To these suggestions I have added another, based on a passage in Richard Wilhelm's *Die Seele Chinas*—a book praised by Hesse—in which there is a striking similarity of ideas and phraseology in the description of a Chinese sage developing into a mummy and lasting into eternity.[35] It is hardly necessary to add that all of these suggestions may be simultaneously valid, in varying degrees, for the language and symbolism of poetry operate on a different plane from that of logic. If the last suggestion be allowed, then this venerable figure, symbolizing unity and saintliness, service in life and in art, also combines the polarities of East and West.

No model has as yet been suggested for Plinio Designori, but his importance in Knecht's life calls at least for a brief comment. He is a "guest pupil" from the outside world and moves through the academic system with Knecht. The two become close friends but engage in repeated debates on the merits of Castalia and the "real" world. Even after Designori returns to political life, in the tradition of his family, he re-enters the novel from time to time; and gradually Knecht, the champion of Castalia, inclines to the world outside, while Designori loses more and more of his Castalian *Heiterkeit* (serenity). Through music and contemplation, Knecht manages to restore a measure of spiritual equanimity in his friend who, in turn, provides the stimulus for Knecht's defection, in order to tutor Designori's "difficult" son Tito. The development of the two protagonists in the novel, Knecht and Designori, represents the central movement toward unity, bridging the abyss between *Geist* and *Leben*. Another portrait included by Hesse[36] is that of his musically gifted nephew Karl Isenberg (Carlo Ferromonte), who helped him especially in his musical studies for the fourth "life" and who, although anti-Nazi to the core, was swept into Hitler's armies and was later listed as missing on the Eastern front.

Naturally, all characters in fiction emanate in some degree from the author, but some are more direct projections than others. Joseph Knecht is obviously close to his creator, but he is not a deliberate, playful, ironic self-portrait, as are Chattus Calvensis II and the "Chinese Elder Brother," who is "a frail man, clothed in gray-yellow linen, spectacles over his blue, patient but expectant eyes" (VI, 207). However, as Boulby states, this "Chinese mask" is more than a bit of *chinoiserie*, a playful ironic adornment, for "the episode of the Elder Brother is in fact central to an understanding of the book." [37] China became for Hesse "a spiritual refuge and second home" (VII, 419). But this Taoist mystic in the bamboo grove is the outsider within the gates of Castalia. The phrase "Elder Brother," while a Chinese form of polite address, is no doubt used as the sign of a hidden relationship and, according to Jung, it is a form of manifestation of the "shadow," the neglected self.[38]

The Castalians admire the rational Confucian strain, whereas Tao is a mystical element in Chinese thought, leading to individualism. The fact that the Elder Brother—the stranger within the gates of Castalia—becomes Knecht's guru is a veiled hint of the element within Knecht that strains away from Castalian ideals. The *Book of Changes*, the *I Ging*, familiar to Hesse in Richard Wilhelm's translation (1924), produces an oracle on Knecht's future, part of which runs "above the mountain, below the water" (VI, 210). J. C. Middleton interprets this to presage the scene of Knecht's death.[39] The Elder Brother's words "initiate more strongly than ever before the theme of service, linking it with inward independence, and indicating the possibility of a loftier ideal than Castalia can provide. . . . Knecht goes that Way his master did not wish to go. . . . But perhaps the way up and the way down are not so totally antithetical after all. When we recall who the Elder Brother really is (or *almost* is), the irony suddenly becomes bottomless."[40]

Joseph Knecht combines aspects represented in most of the peripheral figures. He has within him the capacity for the contemplative and for the active life, as he is attracted both to Tegularius and the Chinese Brother on the one hand, and to Designori and Jacobus on the other. He respects the ascetic Castalian rules forbidding creativity, but composes poems. He is attracted to the austere, lonely scholar's life, but accepts onerous service and responsibility in the hierarchy. He is aware of the past and the future. He yearns for permanence and yet his most characteristic trait is his readiness for change, for metamorphosis. He possesses, in fact, the Faustian quality of striving, for which Hesse uses the leitmotival words *Erwachen* (awakening) and *Stufen* (steps). As in Goethe's *Faust,* this striving transcends even death and is strikingly summarized in Knecht's poem "Stufen":

> Es wird vielleicht auch noch die Todesstunde
> Uns neuen Räumen jung entgegensenden,
> Des Lebens Ruf an uns wird niemals enden . . .
> Wohlan denn, Herz, nimm Abschied und gesunde! [41]

René Dermine saw these Faustian elements in Knecht, but concluded that the *magister ludi* is more a Goethean than a Faustian figure, since he combines, in fruitful bipolarity, aspects of Faust and Wilhelm Meister:

Hesse has dared to combine Faust and Wilhelm Meister in the same being, because he found them combined without contradiction in Goethe himself. . . . Goethe always strove again and again to attain the highest, and that alone seems important to our author. This is true also for Joseph Knecht, and in this respect Goethe was able to serve as a model for him.[42]

With all his inner conflicts and polarities, Joseph Knecht may be summed up in the words used by Conrad Ferdinand Meyer in reference to Ulrich von Hutten: "Er ist ein Mensch mit seinem Widerspruch" ("He is a human being with all his contradictions").

IV   The Poems and Conjectural "Autobiographies" of the Student Knecht

The writing of imaginary autobiographies is a pedagogic exercise required of all Castalian pupils. We recall that in 1925 Hesse, too, had written a "conjectural autobiography," in which he had let his poetic imagination soar into fantastic realms in predicting his future life (*Kurzgefasster Lebenslauf*, IV, 469–89). It may be assumed, however, that Knecht's "lives" exceeded Castalian norms in imagination and poetic coloration. The writing of poems, on the other hand, was definitely forbidden in the Order, and by the very act of composing them Knecht gives evidence at an early age of the anti-Castalian elements in his nature.

The poems themselves, whatever their esthetic merit, provide pithy formulations of the major themes and motifs of the novel. The first, "Klage" ("Lament"), reveals the yearning for permanence within transience and thus reflects the poles of Knecht's being and of the world portrayed in the novel:

> Uns ist kein Sein vergönnt. Wir sind nur Strom,
> Wir fliessen willig allen Formen ein:
> Dem Tag, der Nacht, der Höhle und dem Dom,
> Wir gehn hindurch, uns treibt der Durst nach Sein.
>
> . . . .
>
> Einmal zu Stein erstarren! Einmal dauern!
> Danach ist unsre Sehnsucht ewig rege.[43]

Likewise, the third poem begins with a utopian depiction of the Castalian life, "Anmutig, geistig, arabeskenzart . . ." ("Gracefully, spiritually and delicate like arabesques"), but ends with

the confession: "Doch heimlich dürsten wir nach Wirklichkeit,/
Nach Zeugung und Geburt, nach Leid und Tod" ("But secretely
we thirst for reality, for procreation and birth, for suffering
and death"). It reflects, therefore, not only the same polarity, but
also foreshadows the death of Knecht in the "real" world.
Another poem speaks of the insight "that everything must rot,
wither, and die." Yet "above this nauseous vale of corpses . . .
Geist . . . spreads its glowing lantern, full of yearning, conquers
death and makes itself immortal" (VI, 547).

"Zu einer Toccata von Bach" seems to point to the unifying
theme of music in the novel, for it awakens both *Trieb*
(instinct) and *Geist*. "Ein Traum" suggests the transience of
individual authors and works, but books, in general, remain.
This vision almost certainly influenced the similar scene in the
archives in Hermann Kasack's novel *Die Stadt hinter dem Strom.*
A stanza in "Dienst" strongly points to Knecht's service to
Geist, and to the passing of the torch from one individual to
the next:

> Doch niemals starb des wahren Lebens Ahnung,
> Und unser ist das Amt, im Niedergang
> Durch Zeichenspiel, durch Gleichnis und Gesang
> Fortzubewahren heiliger Ehrfurcht Mahnung.[44]

We have already alluded to the importance of "Stufen," which
gives the strongest formulation of the theme of metamorphosis.
There may be in it also a hint of the theme of reincarnation,
if only in the vague sense of the continuity of *Geist,* and it is
this poem which glorifies Knecht's progressive "stages," transformations, and his repeated "awakenings." This poem will engage
our attention in the next section.

Of the three conjectural autobiographies included in the
novel, *Der Regenmacher* (*The Rainmaker*) is the most revealing
for the interpretation of Knecht's life and of the major themes
of the work. By projecting his incarnation into a primitive
stone-age matriarchal village, Knecht points to the theme of
unity. At the dawn of history, *Geist* was not yet separated from
life. The rainmaker speculates and explores the relationships of
the moon and the stars, but his knowledge is of service to the
community in determining the propitious time for sowing. The
unprecedented drought and famine foreshadow the crisis con-

fronting Castalia later, in Knecht's real life. Having assured the continuity of service to *Geist* through his successor Turu, the rainmaker willingly accepts his role of sacrificial victim, knowing that this is necessary in the service of *Leben* as well as of *Geist*.

In the second "life," we shift to the patristic era of the early church. Josephus Famulus (Servant) becomes a holy hermit to whom penitents flock in the desert, because of his capacity for inspiring confidence and for listening gently and kindly. His reputation reaches another hermit of opposite character, Dion Pugil, who deals rigorously and penetratingly with supplicants. Pugil "was a great judge, punisher, and orderer: he imposed penances, chastisements, and pilgrimages, founded marriages, compelled enemies to make peace, and his authority resembled that of a bishop" (VI, 609). In other words, the two hermits represent the *vita contemplativa* and *vita activa* respectively. Simultaneously, both are filled with a feeling of inadequacy and set out to seek the other. Josephus Famulus "had left a post for which he no longer felt competent" (VI, 614). They meet at an oasis, and each recognizes in the other his necessary counterpart. They spend the rest of their lives jointly in the service of both *Geist* and humanity. Thus we see clearly prefigured the motif of Knecht's defection from Castalia and his quest for completeness and oneness and for a life of service to *Leben* as well as *Geist*.

Of the three "lives," the "Indian Life" is the most Eastern in spirit, although *Der Beichtvater* also alludes to oriental spiritualization and to yoga, which indirectly influenced the early church despite an official ban. Knecht uses the pseudonym Dasa, which suggests "servant" (Ramdas as an Indian name="servant of Rama"). Prominent here is the motif of meditation in the holy hermit whom Dasa serves in the jungle. Equally prominent is the picture of the rapidly changing wheel of fortune, which pitches Dasa to the summit of bliss and honors and then with his defeat and the death of his son to the most abject despair. But this kaleidoscope of life's vicissitudes turns out to be a dream, Samsara, and Dasa awakens to fulfill the simple task of bringing a bowl of water to the holy man: "It was a service which had been asked of him; it was a commission which could be accepted and carried out. It was better than sitting and planning methods of suicide. In any case, obeying and serving were easier and better, and far more innocent and becoming than governing and bearing responsibility" (VI, 684-85). Dasa's menial task and his abnegation of the role of king anticipate Knecht's subsequent actions in laying down his office to accept the humble office of tutor.

There remains the fourth "life," which was not incorporated in the completed work and which has since been published in two unfinished versions.[45] Only the second version uses the first-person-narrative style common to the fiction of these projections. Knecht is here depicted in early eighteenth-century Württemberg, in an environment of vigorous theological and pietist thought—and music. He leaves the ministry to accept a modest post as organist, having discovered in Bach one who transcended differentiation and in his music experienced union with the highest.

Ziolkowski has drawn attention to the sources used by Hesse and to the difficulty of accommodating this historical "incarnation" with the legendary and imaginative ones.[46] He also attempts to use this material to argue for his thesis that Hesse's basic concept shifted, during the composition of the novel, away from the initial utopianism. Boulby denies this and points to the thematic differences in this Württemberg "life," which fits ill with the novel and the other autobiographies.[47] For one thing, the story is atypical in its inversion of the usual roles of father and mother. But more important, the defection from "spirit" is to "music," and this does not prefigure the problem which Knecht faces in the novel. Some of the material did, however, find its way into the finished novel, notably into the chapter entitled "Legende," and the musical studies, which Hesse undertook in 1934 with Karl Isenberg specifically for this unused "life," ultimately came to permeate the whole thematic structure and meaning of the work.

V *The Meaning of Music in* Das Glasperlenspiel

We have already observed the importance of music in Hesse's works, but in *Das Glasperlenspiel* this art plays a much more substantial role, running through the entire novel and carrying its major themes. The beginnings of the Glass-Bead-Game and of Castalia are traced back to the rediscovery, in the "Feuilleton Age," of sixteenth-to-eighteenth-century music in the unadulterated purity of its original conception. One of the central aspects of the "game" is the unifying principle, enabling all arts and all knowledge to be applied to a central theme. As we have seen in *Der Steppenwolf*, music, by its ability to do two or more things simultaneously and to penetrate beyond words directly to the inner mystery, offers an analogy to the "game." But music goes beyond this, for it is a barometer of social and political conditions and offers a guide and model to the moral life.[48]

In the introductory chapter, with its grim picture of our disintegrating civilization, music plays a symptomatic role. Hesse sees nothing of value achieved in music of the modern era, since even the works of the "Immortals," Bach and Mozart, are disfigured in performance by the effort to gain emotional mass appeal through dynamic effects. In our time, productivity in music as in the other arts ends in utter anarchy, the breakdown of all forms, leaving only the meaningless chaos of dynamism *per se*. But in reaction against the trend of the times, a few individuals penetrate to the spirit of the classical composers. From these beginnings, the Glass-Bead-Game arises to become the magnetic pole around which the life of the cultural elite of Castalia revolves. It is significant that music and mathematics were predominant in its genesis, for music, according to Schopenhauer, is the dynamic will itself which is constantly striving to break the bonds of form and return to its primal state of chaotic energy. But Hesse clamps upon the would-be formless energy of music a Kantian moral will, in the guise of mathematics, the most formal, rational, and precise manifestation of human intelligence. Thus in Hesse's novel, music, which in Schopenhauer and Thomas Mann represents a demonic force, is bridled and made the servant and subtle instrument of intellect, *Geist*.

Whereas Mann's musician, Leverkühn, strides onward in the tormenting spiral of heightened creativity under demonic auspices, Hesse's music is, perforce, sterile, for his Castalians eschew creativity. For Hesse, genuine music is to be found only in the sixteenth, seventeenth, and eighteenth centuries, where it is marked by emphasis on the fugue and on counterpoint. This music underwent an almost miraculous development in the hands of Monteverdi, Purcell, Scarlatti, Bach, Handel, Haydn, and Mozart, and finally expressed the ultimate human moral values.

Das Glasperlenspiel

One of the key terms used by Hesse to convey the essential meaning of "genuine" music in its moral connotations is *Heiterkeit*. Any translation of this noun necessarily loses some of the important overtones. "Serenity" suggests calm, quiescence, passivity, omitting all reference to activity, responsiveness, cheerfulness, and gaiety, all of which connotations the term adumbrates. Another important constituent is "balance." *Heiterkeit* denotes the transcending of dissensions, such as the conflict between *Geist* and *Leben* or mind and matter, and implies a happy equilibrium.

In a letter written in 1934, Hesse quotes the Chinese sage Lü Pu Wei in a dictum which later found its way into *Das Glasperlenspiel:* "Perfect music has its cause. It is borne of equilibrium. Equilibrium arises from a meaningful universe. Hence one can talk of music only with one who has perceived the meaning of the universe" (VII, 571). It is no coincidence that the perfect music of the eighteenth century found its fulfillment in the age of rationalism and humanism, of the moral philosophers Shaftesbury and Leibniz, and in an ordered, harmonious universe (in the mind, if not in reality). Obversely, it is obvious that to Hesse the world of today is meaningless and chaotic, and that, for him, contemporary music reflects this anarchic state and has lost its virtue as moral symbol and guide.

This degeneration of moral and political life is mirrored in the debasement of genuine music, which is replaced by a false dynamic expression lacking all *Heiterkeit*:

Lü Pu Wei is informed on Wagner, too, the pied piper and favorite composer of the second German Empire, and still more of the Third Reich: "The more Saturnalian the music, the more dangerous becomes the nation, the deeper sinks the ruler," etc. Or: "Such music is intoxicating, to be sure, but it has departed from the nature of true music. Therefore it is not serene [*heiter*]. If music is not serene, the populace grumbles and a blight descends upon life" and "The music of a well-ordered age is controlled and cheerful [*ruhig* and *heiter*] and the regime equable. The music of an uneasy epoch is excited and excessive and its regime is awry. The music of a decaying state is sentimental and its regime is imperiled." [49]

In the well-ordered world of the Castalian elite, the spirit of seventeenth- and eighteenth-century music reigns supreme. The Glass-Bead-Game itself is a sort of improvisation in which "genuine" musical themes are "played" in variations architectural, mathematical, poetical, etc., comprising a sort of encyclopedic counterpoint of all the arts and sciences. It has developed, we are told, "into a sublime cult, a *unio mystica* of all the discrete members of the *universitas litterarum.*" Like eighteenth-century music, it is a subtle combination of fancy and suggestion with strict formal control. But it is not merely the cultural institution of the game which is an extension of the spirit of this music. The Castalian Order and its way of life represent the transference of the values of this music into daily life and social and political intercourse. The Castalian historian declares that the "Glasperlenspiel" is basically a "playing of music" (*Musizieren*) in the sense of the words once spoken by Joseph Knecht on the meaning of classical music:

"We consider classical music the essence and epitome of our culture, because it is its most meaningful and most characteristic expression and gesture. We possess in this music the legacy of the ancient world and of Christendom, a spirit of cheerful and courageous devotion, an unexcelled code of chivalrous conduct. For in the last resort, every classical gesture of a civilization signifies a moral code, a model of human conduct contracted into a gesture. Between 1500 and 1800, many kinds of music have been composed, and the styles and means of expression were most diverse, but the spirit—rather the morality—is everywhere the same. The human attitude expressed in classical music is always identical; it is always based on the same kind of supremacy over chance. The gesture of classical music signifies: an awareness of human tragedy, the acceptance of man's fate, courage, and *Heiterkeit*. Whether it be the grace of a minuet by Handel or Couperin, or sensuality sublimated into a delicate gesture, as in many Italians or in Mozart, or the calm readiness for death, as in Bach, there is always in it a challenge, a deathless courage, a breath of chivalry and an echo of superhuman laughter, of immortal *Heiterkeit*. Thus it shall ring out in our 'glass-bead-games' and in all our life, work, and suffering." (VI, 116)

Joseph Knecht becomes increasingly aware of the defects and dangers threatening Castalia. They result from a spreading hubris among the human beings who comprise the Castalian world: the assumption that their world is static, perfect, complete, in a state of *Sein* (being). But the human vessels and institutions serving *Geist* are themselves inevitably involved in the historical process, in *Werden* (becoming). This process can only be retrograde when men and institutions are morally unprepared to face the repeated challenge.

It is music that brings Knecht to this insight, for music is engaged in a constant battle with the material forces of dissolution, chaos, and anarchy, struggling to subject matter to form. There is, however, another quality of music which is even more enlightening to Knecht; for music is itself change, process, "becoming," the very opposite of *Sein*. It fills space and time, to which it gives form and meaning, but without ever lingering. It must constantly surge forward, bringing light to darkness, meaning to senseless matter. This musical analogy, Knecht later realizes, subconsciously underlay his poem "Transzendieren," which he later modestly rechristened "Stufen" ("Steps"). In the later crises of his life, Knecht recalls these lines:

> Wir sollen heiter Raum um Raum durchschreiten,
> An keinem wie an einer Heimat hängen,
> Der Weltgeist will nicht fesseln uns und engen,
> Er will uns Stuf' um Stufe heben, weiten.

> (Serene and full of cheer we spur the chase
> And ever onward stride through time and space
> And nowhere cling as to a home of yesteryear.
> The *Weltgeist* seeks not to restrain and tie:
> His purpose is to raise and magnify
> Us stage by stage beyond the hemisphere.)

This moral lesson derived from music—the necessity of change and rebirth, and the transience of the material things of life, of man and his institutions—is reinforced by another aspect of this art: its embodiment of *Geist*, which is eternal and finds its expression in all human beings and their achievements. Another of Knecht's poems closes with the lines:

> Denn auch in uns lebt Geist vom ewigen Geist,
> Der aller Zeiten Geister Brüder heisst:
> *Er* überlebt das Heut, nicht Du und Ich.

(For in us, too, lives the spirit of the eternal spirit that is kin with the spirits of all ages: It is this spirit which survives the transitory moment, not you and I.)

Early in his life, Knecht had been awakened to the presence of *Geist* when, as a boy, he heard the old "Musikmeister" improvise a fugue for him. As he had listened to the message of *Geist*, he had resolved to dedicate his life to its service: "It seemed to him as if today he were hearing music for the first time. Behind the musical edifice that arose before him, he felt the spirit (*Geist*), the beneficient harmony of law and liberty, of serving and swaying; he surrendered and dedicated himself to this spirit and this master" (VI, 126).

Music suggests the brotherhood of man through the potential participation of each human soul in the universal and eternal *Geist*, and it suggests that the individual's dedication to the service of *Geist* can and also should be devotion to the service of his fellow man. When Knecht faces the final crisis of his life—the apparent conflict between his duty to the rarefied form of *Geist* cultivated by the Castalians on the one side and his duty to mankind on the other—he has a long conversation with his friend from the outside world, Designori. He tells Designori that the genuine "Glasperlenspieler" (i.e. artist or intellectual) "should, above all, possess the *Heiterkeit* of music, which is, after all, nothing else but courage, a serene, smiling, striding, and dancing onward, right through the horrors and flames of the world, the solemn and festive offering of a sacrifice" (VI, 420). To emphasize the moral lesson inherent in this musical analogy, Knecht sits down and plays for his friend a movement from the Purcell sonata which had been a favorite piece of Pater Jacobus:

Like drops of golden light, the sounds descended in the stillness, so softly that between them could still be heard the song of the old spring murmuring in the courtyard. Gently and insistently, temperately and sweetly, the voices of the gracious music met and entwined with one another; bravely and serenely they paced out their intimate dance through the nothingness of time and transitoriness and for the short spell of their duration made the space and the nocturnal hour as wide and infinite as the universe. (VI, 421)

Like Purcell's music, Joseph Knecht strides on, brave and serene, into the world of chaos and transience, and in thus dedicating himself to the dual service of the eternal *Geist* and ever-changing man, his life is not in vain. As he succumbs in the icy water of the mountain lake, his message—the message of *Geist* itself and of service to humanity—takes hold and glows, never to be extinguished, in the heart and mind of his pupil Tito. Just as the notes of Purcell's music filled the stillness "like drops of golden light" and danced their way bravely and serenely through the emptiness of transient time, so young Tito catches the glow of *Geist* in his master Knecht and dances in the golden light of the sun rising over the mountain rim. This, we are told, was not a dance familiar to him, nor was it invented by him as a rite to celebrate the sunrise. Only later was he to realize that his dance and his trance-like enthusiasm had been occasioned not merely by the mountain air, the sun, and the early morning feeling of freedom, but even more by the transformation and impending development in his young life, heralded by the impact of the friendly but venerable figure of the former *magister ludi,* Joseph Knecht. Thus it is implied that the *Geist* which is manifest in music, and which is epitomized in the Purcell sonata, is carried over into life, into Knecht's life of serenity and service, and after him into the life of young Tito.

Music is the key to the role of Knecht, and that of his pupil Tito, in the interpenetration of life and intellect, *Leben* and *Geist.* Its normative moral character is brought out most clearly in the life and death of the *Altmusikmeister,* who is the guiding spirit in Knecht's life. While still alive, this "music master" is transfigured and translated into virtual sainthood:

It was a life of devotion and labor, but free from compulsion and ambition, and full of music. And it seemed as if, by becoming a musician and *Musikmeister,* he had chosen music as one of the ways to the highest goal of mankind, to inner freedom, purity, and perfection, and as if, since choosing this path, he had done nothing but let himself become more and more penetrated, transfigured, and purified by music, from the clever, skilled harpsichordist's hands and teeming, titanic musician's memory into all parts of his body and soul, even to his pulse and breathing, even in his sleeping and dreaming, and that now he was a virtual symbol, or rather an embodiment, a personification of music. (VI, 356)

Hesse's music, "genuine" music, has, then, a preeminently moral connotation. It has a rational basis and a formative, ordering character. It is both symbolic of the meaning and purpose of human life and of man's relationship to the things of the spirit, while, at the same time, being a concrete guide to moral action and the virtuous life. The life of the *Altmusik-*

meister is one of devotion and service to music, and through music he serves the highest aims of mind and spirit and, at the same time, exemplifies the highest virtues in life. His life under the aegis of music is a constant progression on the path to sainthood. The "music master" is referred to as Knecht's "guardian angel," "spiritual mentor," "ideal model" and *"Daimonion"*—a word evocative of Demian (VI, 117,171,309). When Hesse was asked whether he regarded Knecht as a Christ-like figure, he denied this, adding: "In Knecht I would rather see a brother of the saints. There are many of them . . . they are the 'elite' of cultures and world history, and they are distinguished from 'ordinary' human beings through the fact that they achieve subordination and devotion to something suprapersonal, not because of a lack of personality and originality, but through a plus of individuality." [50]

Hesse's comment clearly illuminates the polarity exemplified in Knecht's life. He reaches the pinnacle of the hierarchy and presides with the greatest effectiveness, just because of the anti-hierarchical, polar tensions within him, which he has the strength to control as long as his hierarchical role seems justified. When it becomes problematical, he is ready for a new "awakening." Classical music and the exemplary figure of the "music master" provide clues to his nature and to his greatness or "saintliness." Knecht's life, like that of the *Altmusikmeister,* is a progressive apotheosis and a continuous development, through "awakenings" or metamorphoses, toward the service of both *Geist* and *Leben.*

CHAPTER 11

Conclusion

IN calling Hermann Hesse "the last knight of Romanticism," Hugo Ball contributed to a misunderstanding of his place in literature, for this phrase was caught up and echoed by many critics. It represents, of course, a certain truth, but only a partial one. Far from denying his indebtedness to Romantic literature, Hesse himself emphasized its importance for his work; and, indeed, he made it his special task to rehabilitate Jean Paul, finally publishing a new edition of that arch-Romantic.

But Hugo Ball's phrase has an unfortunate ring that suggests that Hesse faced the past. Thomas Mann judged far more perceptively when he wrote that Hesse had produced a more *avant-garde* work in *Der Steppenwolf* than Gide had in *The Counterfeiters*. He went on to say that the best servitors of the new are those who do not discard the old but carry it forward, transformed, into the present and future. This, of course, is characteristic also of Thomas Mann; and this awareness, no doubt, was instrumental in bringing these two writers together spiritually, despite their disparate origins and development. Of both Hesse and Mann it may be said that they are Janus-faced—Mann with deep roots in the nineteenth century and Hesse rooted even further back in the eighteenth. While looking at the past, they faced the present and the future, applying and using inherited forms, but experimenting with them, developing them further, and filling them with the problematical content of the present.

André Gide observed that in Hesse's works only the expression is tempered—but not the feeling and the thought.[1]

Many honors came to Hesse in his later years, including the Nobel Prize for Literature in 1946, which was bestowed upon him for his whole work, of course, but particularly for *Das Glasperlenspiel*. He received the Goethe Prize of the city of Frankfurt in the same year, the Wilhelm Raabe Prize of Bremen in 1950, and the Peace Prize of the German Book Trade in 1955. In 1947 he was given an honorary doctorate by the University of Berne and in 1955 he was awarded the Order Pour le mérite. But he never left his Swiss retreat and accepted these tributes with the lifelong modesty and humility which was one of his endearing characteristics and which is so prominent a trait in his Joseph Knecht.

Of Hesse's permanent place in twentieth-century literature there can be little doubt. How many of his works will remain standard texts is a more problematical question, but probably all his major works of fiction from *Demian* to *Das Glasperlenspiel* will remain literary landmarks.

In the years since his death in 1962, interest in Hesse has increased rather than diminished. While this is true of the German-speaking world, it is even more strikingly demonstrated in America and, to a lesser extent, in the other English-speaking countries. But part of the current enthusiasm rests on a dubious basis and may be short-lived. For the Hippie generation has adopted him and, probably for the wrong reasons, sees in him mainly the "outsider," the nonconformist rebel against standardized norms and conventions. This side of Hesse is, of course, especially striking in the works of the middle period—*Demian, Siddhartha, Der Steppenwolf*—but is considerably mellowed in *Die Morgenlandfahrt* and *Das Glasperlenspiel*. For in later years Hesse increasingly appreciated the values of tradition and the importance of the impersonal and suprapersonal in life and art. Even as early as *Der Steppenwolf* and *Narziss und Goldmund*, the voice of the outsider was countered by that of the opposite tendency: the Immortals and the hierarchy of Narziss, for both Mozart and Narziss fundamentally represent *Geist;* and Hesse's final vision is one of harmony between centrifugal, "outsider" forces and centripetal forces of cohesion. Ultimately, the individual who is the personal, fragile bearer of *Geist* is called to service and sacrifice.

Notes and References

Hesse's works are cited from the collected edition wherever possible: *Gesammelte Schriften* (*G.S.*), 7 vols. (Frankfurt: Suhrkamp, 1958). Parenthetical references in the text give volume and page. I have used my own translations throughout.

Chapter One

1. Mark Boulby, *Hermann Hesse: His Mind and Art* (Ithaca, 1967), p. 9.
2. Quoted in Hugo Ball, *Hermann Hesse: Sein Leben und sein Werk* (Zürich, 1947), pp. 16–17.
3. Bernhard Zeller, *Hermann Hesse* (Hamburg, 1963), p. 18.
4. *Kurzgefasster Lebenslauf, G.S.*, IV, 471–72.
5. Zeller, *op. cit.*, p. 12.
6. Cf. Knecht's poem *"Stufen," G.S.*, VI, 555.

Chapter Two

1. Quoted in *Zeller, op, cit.*, p. 36.
2. Dances and dangers sank into the dark river of time; without seams, without limits the arc of my solitude extends in space. Green and gold and heaven disappeared; over the shores of my sick soul lies the land of my nostalgia.
3. *Neue Zürcher Zeitung*, August 4, 1951.
4. Passage omitted in *G.S.* but found on p. 114 of the Fischer edition, Berlin, 1925.
5. Ninon Hesse, ed., *Kindheit und Jugend vor Neunzehnhundert. Hermann Hesse in Briefen und Lebenszeugnissen 1877–1895* (Frankfurt, 1966).
6. *Ibid.*, pp. 325–326.
7. I, 465. For the unexpurgated version cf. 1906 edition.
8. Boulby, p. 52.

9. *Ibid*, p. 63.

10. *Pour l'art*, Lausanne-Paris, No. 61 (July-August, 1958), p. 37.

Chapter Three

1. *Prosa aus dem Nachlass*, ed. Ninon Hesse (Frankfurt, 1965).

2. Muoth is of course Bavarian and archaic for *Mut* (= courage), the quality exemplified in the singer who must fight obstacles within and without to project his role day after day. The name Kuhn is an unumlauted variant of *kühn* (= bold) and reminds one of Adrian Leverkühn (live boldly) with its Nietzschean echo. Hesse's Kuhn, however, is ambivalent. Taken in the Nietzschean sense the implication would be ironic, for he is a shrinking violet facing life. On the other hand, it is possible to see "boldness" in his impetus to pursue art without restraint.

3. *Aus Indien* (Berlin, 1919), p. 113 (not in *G.S.*).

4. Quoted in Zeller, p. 67.

5. A curious anticipation of the fate destined to befall Hesse's youngest son Martin in 1915. Martin, however, survived the crisis of this disease, and the parents were temporarily reunited over the painful spasms of their little son.

6. Adele Lewisohn, *Gertrude and I*, after the German of *Gertrud* (New York, 1915). A new translation by Hilda Rosner appeared in London, 1955.

7. For evidence of bad translation see my article "Hermann Hesse: A Neglected Nobel Prize Novelist," *Queen's Quarterly*, LXV (1958), pp. 514–20.

Chapter Four

1. *Krieg und Frieden* (Zürich, 1946). Some of the same items are contained in *Betrachtungen*.

2. Hermann Hesse–Romain Rolland, *Briefe* (Zürich, 1954).

3. Theodore Ziolowski, *The Novels of Hermann Hesse: A Study in Theme and Structure* (Princeton, 1965), cf. esp. pp. 109–18, 133–38.

4. Malte Dahrendorf, "Hermann Hesses *Demian* und C. G. Jung," *Germanisch-Romanische Monatsschrift*, XXXIX (1958), 81–97. Cf. also the same author's "Hermann Hesses *Demian*," *Staatsexamensarbeit*, Hamburg, 1953.

5. Boulby, pp. 98–120.

6. Cf. correspondence between E. Maier, Jung, and Hesse published in *The Psychoanalytic Review*, L (1963). On the connection between Hesse and Jung, see also Miguel Serrano, *C. G. Jung and Hermann Hesse: A Record of Two Friendships* (London, 1966).

7. *Symbols of Transformation* (*Collected Works*, V [Bollingen Series XX; New York, 1956]), 124. Subsequent references to this edition appear by page number alone in parentheses in the text.

8. Jolande Jacobi, *The Psychology of C. G. Jung*. 6th ed. revised (London, 1962), p. 112.

9. Nietzsche, *Werke* (Stuttgart: Kröner [Gross- und Klein-Oktavausgabe]), VI, 114.

10. I was an offspring of nature, a throw into the unknown, perhaps destined for what is new, perhaps for extinction, and to let this throw work its way out of the primal depths, to feel its will within me and make it entirely mine, this alone was my calling (III, 221). This passage is a good example of the difficulty of translating Hesse's deceptively simple prose. The thrice repeated "Wurf" has overtones suggesting 1) the individuation process from the collective unconscious, 2) the generative birth process, 3) the cast of dice.

11. Ziolkowski, pp. 140–41.

12. *Ibid.*, p. 144.

13. Joseph Mileck, "Names and the Creative Process," *Monatshefte*, LIII (1961), 167–80.

14. *Die Neue Rundschau*, October, 1919, supplement, p. 7.

Chapter Five

1. Ninon Hesse, *Kindheit und Jugend vor Neunzehnhundert* (Frankfurt, 1966), p. 27.

2. Heinz W. Puppe, "Psychologie und Mystik in *Klein und Wagner* von Hermann Hessse," *PMLA*, LXXVIII (1963), 131.

3. *Ibid.*, p. 132.

4. Death by drowning recurs with astonishing frequency in Hesse's work: Peter's friend Richard in *Peter Camenzind*, Hans Giebenrath in *Unterm Rad*, Joseph Knecht in *Das Glasperlenspiel*. Contemplation of such a death occurs in *Siddhartha* and *Narziss und Goldmund*. Water, of course, has a symbolic, leitmotif function, suggesting oneness, loss of individuation, and submergence in the cosmos, as manifest in *Klein und Wagner* and *Siddhartha*.

5. Hermann Hesse, *Aus einem Tagebuch des Jahres 1920* (Zürich, 1960), p. 38.

6. Ernst Rose, *Faith from the Abyss: Hermann Hesse's Way from Romanticism to Modernity* (New York, 1965), p. 62.

7. Fritz Martini, "Der Expressionsmus" in *Deutsche Literatur im zwanzigsten Jahrhundert,* ed. H. Friedmann and Otto Mann (Heidelberg, 1954), p. 108. For a discussion of the connection between Hesse and Paul Klee see Joyce Hallamore, "Paul Klee, H. H. and *Die Morgenlandfahrt,*" *Seminar,* I (1965), pp. 17–24.

8. The mention of Arles (III, 573) may be taken as a deliberate allusion to van Gogh.

9. Boulby, p. 129.

10. Martini *op cit.,* p. 111.

11. *Ibid.,* p. 113.

12. High up they sat in a soaring swing facing the stars above the abyss of the world and night, birds in a golden cage, homeless, weightless. The birds sang, sang exotic songs, they improvised from the depths of intoxicated hearts into the night, into the heavens, into the forest, into the problematic enchanted universe. Answer came from star and moon, from tree and mountain, Goethe sat there and Hafiz; the hot breath of Egypt was wafted up and the devout air of Greece, Mozart smiled, Hugo Wolf played on the piano in the delirious night. . . . Klingsor, King of the Night, a tall crown in his hair, leaning back on his stone seat, was directing the dance of the world, marking time, calling forth the moon, causing the railway to disappear.

[Amid the wild fancy there is in the last words a key to the immediate setting: beneath Montagnola the railway from Lugano to Milan hugs the shore, then enters a tunnel before crossing the lake on a causeway to enter Italy.]

13. *Die Neue Rundschau,* 1918, pt. 1, p. 841.

Chapter Six

1. *Aus einem Tagebuch des Jahres 1920* (Zürich, 1960), p. 32.

2. *Der Weg nach Innen* (Berlin, 1931).

3. *Vivos voco,* I (1919–20), 72–73.

4. Printed as note 7 in my article "Hermann Hesse as Critic of English and American Literature," *Monatshefte,* LIII (1961), 147–58.

5. *Piktors Verwandlungen,* Faksimile-Ausgabe (Frankfurt, 1954).

6. "Child-people" is a paradoxical term, as Boulby points out: "Their childlikeness both is and is not that spoken of in the New Testament; theirs is the sphere of reality, with which the magical reality can never coincide" (p. 141).

7. *Siddhartha,* ed. T. C. Dunham and A. S. Wensinger, New York, Macmillan, 1962, p. 181. This is an excellent text edition with glossary of Eastern terms.

8. Rudolf Pannwitz, *Hermann Hesses West-östliche Dichtung* (Frankfurt, 1957), p 13.

9. III, 647: Beautiful was the world, many-colored was the world, strange and enigmatic was the world.

10. III, 716: Slowly bloomed, slowly ripened in Siddhartha the insight, the knowledge of the real nature of wisdom, the goal of his long quest. It was nothing but a readiness of the soul, a capacity, a mysterious ability at any moment in the midst of life to be able to think the thought of oneness, to feel and breathe in oneness. Slowly this bloomed in him, radiated back to him from Vasudeva's old, child-like face: harmony, knowledge of the eternal fulfillment of the world, smiling serenity, oneness.

11. *Op. cit.*, pp. 170–77.

12. III, 721: Brightly gleamed Vasudeva's smile, over all the wrinkles of his aged countenance it hovered radiantly, just as over all the voices of the river *om* hovered. Brightly gleamed his smile, as he looked at his friend, and brightly gleamed now on Siddhartha's face, too, the same smile. His wound flourished, his pain shone radiantly, his ego had flowed into the oneness.

13. *Op. cit.*, pp. 160–61.

14. Cf. e.g. "Kurzgefasster Lebenslauf" *G.S.*, IV, 469–89.

15. Ralph Freedman, *The Lyrical Novel: Studies in Hermann Hesse, André Gide and Virginia Woolf* (Princeton, 1963).

Chapter Seven

1. Hesse's works, especially *Der Steppenwolf*, were a major influence in Colin Wilson's *The Outsider: An Inquiry into the Nature of the Sickness of Mankind in the mid-twentieth Century*. (London, 1956). This book is not to be recommended without reservation since it is full of errors, mistranslations, and misinterpretations, but it does present the basic theme with flamboyance.

2. Soon, when I am drunk again, an automobile will come running along and with sure hand wheel me to death. He too, I hope, will break his neck in the process, this happy Catholic, possessor of house, factory, and garden, for whom two children and a wife are waiting and who would have earned still more money and begotten more children, if a drunken poet had not run between his headlights.

3. Everything is leaving me in the lurch. Now my love too is broken. It was so horrible. She was called Erika Maria Ruth. I listened long to her open lips, but there was no breath and no sound! And no heartbeat under the ribs; everything had escaped and was gone. Now there is no more quarreling and love. Oh, abandoned soul that I am, I have crushed this blossom, too. Everything is void, I wish I

were dead, I wish I were the knife with which I stabbed her to death. The blood on the floor had congealed in a dark mass; I remained standing in it long. But from all the extinguished suns there was no evening glow, not a glimmer to be seen. I tore it [in German ambiguous= "her," "them"] down from Heaven and with my hands smashed it to bits. That's the way it all had to end, with these bloody blanched hands. . . .

4. *Demian*, tr. N. H. Friday (New York, 1948).

5. Quoted by Fritz Strich in "Dank an Hermann Hesse" in *Der Dichter und die Zeit* (Berne, 1947), pp. 377–94.

6. Ziolkowski, p. 178.

7. For some of this material I am indebted to R. H. Farquharson's unpublished dissertation "The Development of the Love Theme in the Works of Hermann Hesse," Univ. of California (Berkeley, 1962).

8. *Handwörterbuch des deutschen Aberglaubens* (Leipzig, 1936–37), VIII, 18.

9. *The Custom of the Country*, Act V, Sc. 1.

10. Bürger's defense: "What the rigidity of secular laws would not have allowed, three persons believed themselves permitted to sanction for their mutual salvation from ruin." *Ehestandsgeschichte* (Berlin, 1812), pp. 46–47.

11. This and the following paragraphs are adapted from my article "Music and Morality in Thomas Mann and Hermann Hesse," *University of Toronto Quarterly*, XXIV (1955), pp. 175–90.

12. *Op. cit.*, pp. 178–228.

13. *Ibid.*, pp. 181–82.

14. *Ibid.*, pp. 189–90.

15. Cf. p. 88.

16. *Op. cit.* p. 213.

17. *Ibid.*, p. 216.

18. *Ibid.*, p. 222.

19. Egon Schwarz, "Zur Erklarung von Hesses *Steppenwolf*," *Monatshefte*, LIII (1961), 191–98.

20. Theodore Ziolkowski, "Hermann Hesse's Chiliastic Vision," *Monatshefte*, LIII (1961), 201–202.

21. *Op. cit.*, pp. 200–204.

Chapter Eight

1. Esp. in Max Schmid, *Hermann Hesse: Weg und Wandlung* (Zürich, 1947).

2. Helmut Waibler, *Hermann Hesse, Eine Bibliographie* (Berne and Munich, 1962), p. 39.

Notes and References

3. *Faust I*, 11.2038–39: Gray, dear friend, is all theory, and green is the golden tree of life.

4. Max Schmid, *op. cit.*, p. 107.

5. It has been praised by Joseph Mileck in *Hermann Hesse and His Critics* (Chapel Hill, 1958) and by Ernst Robert Curtius in "Hermann Hesse," *Kritische Essays zur Europäischen Literatur* (Berne, 1950). It has been pilloried (no doubt unfairly) by Karlheinz Deschner in *Kitsch, Konvention und Kunst* (Munich, 1957) and subjected to a very critical interpretation by Ziolkowski (pp. 229–52). Boulby (pp. 207–43) sees certain weaknesses but also claims considerable importance for it.

6. Max Schmid, p. 123.

7. *Op. cit.*, p. 105.

8. In Hugo Ball, *op. cit.*, pp. 257–58.

9. *Berthold. Ein Romanfragment* (Zürich, 1950); *G.S.* I, 831–83.

10. Boulby, *op. cit.*, pp. 215–16.

11. *März* (1908), III, pp. 33–38, 131-37, 225-59, 289–91; *Schweizerland*, VII (1921), 418–29; *Die Neue Rundschau*, XXXIII (1922), 1175–86.

12. Cf. e.g. *Symbols of Transformation:* The father is the representative of the spirit, whose function is to oppose pure instinctuality (p. 261); and the "mother" . . . is the gateway into the unconscious (p. 330).

13. Boulby, *op. cit.*, p. 218, *et passim*.

14. I find it hard to accept Boulby's only specific evidence of carelessness (*op. cit.*, p. 211), namely that "Konrad" should surely read "Adolf" (V, 87), since three fellow pupils have been singled out by name as sharing in the village escapade: Eberhard, Konrad, and Adolf. Any one of the three could enter Goldmund's mind at this point.

15. *Op. cit.*, pp. 119–21.

16. Now the woman smiled at his look of astonishment, smiled in a very friendly way, and slowly he too began to smile. On his smiling lips. . . .

17. Deschner, *op. cit.*, p. 126: Beautiful was life, beautiful and fleeting was happiness, beautiful and quickly withered was youth.

18. Boulby, *op. cit.*, pp. 238–241.

Chapter Nine

1. Joseph Mileck, "The Poetry of Hermann Hesse," *Monatshefte*, XLVI (1954), 192–98.

2. In "Eine Fussreise im Herbst," *Rheinlande*, 6 (1906), *Bd. II*, 59–65.

3. Strange, to wander in the mist. Every bush and stone is sealed off, no tree sees the other, each is alone.
Full of friends was my world, when my life was yet light; now that the mist is falling none is any longer in sight.
Truly, no one is wise who does not know the dark which inexorably and gently separates him from all others.
Strange, to wander in the mist! Life is loneliness. No man knows the other, each is isolated.

4. Ever to and fro strives the blossoming branch in the wind. Ever up and down strives my heart, like a child, between bright and dark days, between willing and renouncing.
Until the blossoms are scattered and the branch is full of fruit, until my heart, satiated with childhood, finds its peace and confesses: full of joy and not in vain was the restless game of life.

5. Max Schmid, *Hermann Hesse: Weg und Wandlung* (Zürich, 1947), pp. 17–25.

6. Joseph Mileck, "The Poetry of Hermann Hesse," *Monatshefte*, XLVI (1954), 193–94.

7. From the tree of life leaf after leaf falls from me. O gay and giddy world, how you sate, how you sate and tire, how you intoxicate! What today still glows will soon be submerged. Soon the wind will clatter over my brown grave, over the little child the mother bends down. Her eyes I would see again, her look is my star, everything else may go and pass away, all dies, all dies gladly. Only the eternal mother remains from whom we came, her playing finger writes in the fleeting air our names.

8. Deschner, *op. cit.*, pp. 146–56.

9. *G.S.*, V, 347. An approximate rendering of the hexameter form: Therefore let us be modest and let us confront events
Even in perilous times with that peacefulness deep in the soul's center
Which the ancients so praised and strove after, let us do good,
Not all at once upsetting the world; this way, too, will reward us.

10. Cf. Richard B. Matzig, *Hermann Hesse. Studien zu Werk und Innenwelt des Dichters* (Stuttgart, 1947), pp. 136–37.

11. Cf. Werner Kohlschmidt, "Meditationen über Hermann Hesses *Glasperlenspiel*," *Zeitwende*, XIX (1947–48), 154–70, 217–26.

12. Horst Kliemann and Karl H. Silomon, *Hermann Hesse, eine bibliographische Studie* (Munich, 1947), p. 73.

13. Divine and eternal is mind and spirit. Toward this force whose image and tool we are, leads our way. Our deepest yearning is to become as it is, to shine in its light.
But we are created mortal and earthen. Heaviness weighs oppressively on us creatures. To be sure, nature embraces us tenderly with maternal

warmth, earth suckles us and beds us down in cradle and grave. But nature does not satisfy us. Its maternal spell is penetrated paternally by the spark of immortal *Geist* and the child is made into a man. Innocence is extinguished, and we are awakened to struggle and conscience.

Thus between mother and father, between matter and mind, vacillates creation's most fragile child, the quivering soul of man, capable of suffering like no other creature, and capable of the highest: believing, hoping, love. Difficult is his path, sin and death his sustenance. Often he errs in darkness, often he would prefer never to have been created. But always he is radiated by his yearning, his destiny: Light, *Geist*. And we feel that the eternal *Geist* loves with particular affection the exposed and imperiled human soul.

Therefore for us erring brothers love is still possible even in our disunion, and not judging and hating but tolerant love, loving tolerance, leads us closer to the sacred goal.

14. Man shall be noble, helpful and good! "Das Göttliche" ("The Divine").

15. *Akzente* (October, 1962) and *Hermann Hesse zum Gedächtnis,* Private edition, ed. Siegfried Unseld.

16. Broken branch, still rocking by splintered strands, leafless and without bark. I saw it hanging like that year after year. Its groaning laments in every wind.

That's the way groans and laments echo in the bones of men who have lived too long. One is crippled, not yet severed, one groans whenever a breath quivers.

I harken long to your song, to the fibrous, dry, old branch. It sounds vexed and somewhat anxious, what you, like me, have to announce in groans.

17. Splintered, crippled branch, hanging year after year, drily it groans its song in the wind, without leaves, without bark, bald, blanched, tired of too long living, of too long dying. Its song sounds hard and tough, sounds defiant, sounds secretly anxious, one more summer, one more winter long.

18. This passage is adapted from my published note in *The German Quarterly,* XXXVII (1964), 100–101.

19. Hesse seems to have had similar feelings. In a letter to Thomas Mann of April 26, 1942, he comments on the preparation of a volume of his collected poems: "In the process it was established that I had written some eleven thousand lines of verse. I was appalled to no small degree at this number."

20. *Menschliches, Allzumenschliches,* section 171.

21. Horst Kliemann, "Hermann Hesse und das Buch: Bemerkungen zu einer Hesse-Bibliographie," *Deutsche Beiträge,* I

(1947), p. 6. Bernhard Zeller mentions an incomplete card index for the years 1920–1938 kept by Hesse, which shows that he reviewed 1,160 books in this period. *Hermann Hesse: Neue deutsche Bücher* (Marbach, 1965), p. 142.

22. Hesse's critical writings have not received the attention they deserve. Among those aware of his achievement in this field is Bernhard Zeller, who speaks of the astonishing "sureness, independence and incorruptibility with which in the flood of each year's new publications, the essential and lasting was recognized, culled, and characterized with simple and clear words" (*loc. cit.*, p. 143). Horst Kliemann states that Hesse "had placed himself in the front rank of German critics—a fact that is far too little known" ("Hermann Hesse und das Buch: Bemerkungen zu einer Hesse-Bibliographie" [*Deutsche Beitrage* I (1947), p. 7]. Thomas Mann declared that Hesse's essay on Goethe's *Wilhelm Meister* was "the warmest and cleverest that has been written about the novel since Friedrich Schlegel" (*Hermann Hesse–Thomas Mann: Briefwechsel* [Frankfurt, 1968], p. 122).

23. *Die Neue Rundschau*, XLII (1935), pp. 665–66.

24. G. W. Field, "Hermann Hesse as Critic of English and American Literature," *Monatshefte*, LIII (1961), pp. 147–58; Peter B. Gontrum "Hermann Messe as a Critic of French Literature," *Symposium*, XIX (1965), pp. 226–35; Vasa D. Mihailovich, "Hermann Hesse as a Critic of Russian Literature," *Arcadia*, II (1967), pp. 91–102. Some of the material in this chapter has appeared in my essay mentioned above.

25. *Die Neue Rundschau* (1947), repr. in *H. H.–Th. M.: Briefwechsel* (Frankfurt, 1968), p. 132.

26. *Gullivers Reisen*, tr. Carl Seelig, intr. Hermann Hesse (Leipzig, 1923; repr. Zürich, 1955)

27. *Die Neue Rundschau*, 1934, pt. 1, p. 458.

28. *Ibid.*, 1933 (May), insert, p. 2.

29. *März*, 1909, II, 57.

30. For Whitman see *Propyläen*, 1904–1905, p. 99; for Poe, *Vivos Voco*, 1921–22, p. 706.

31. *Die Neue Rundschau*, 1933 (June), insert, pp. 6–7.

32. *Ibid.*, 1929, pt. 2, p. 413.

33. *Die Weltwoche*, Dec. 24, 1953.

34. *Briefwechsel* (Frankfurt, 1968), pp. 123–24.

35. *Ibid.*, pp. 111–12.

36. Unpublished Diary in *Nachlass*, Schiller-Nationalmuseum.

37. *Briefwechsel* (Frankfurt, 1968), p. 18.

38. Bernhard Zeller, ed., *Hermann Hesse: Neue deutsche Bücher. Literaturberichte für Bonniers Litterära Magasin 1935–1936* (Marbach, Schiller-Nationalmuseum, 1965).

39. Quoted in *ibid.*, pp. 147–48.
40. Hermann Hesse, "Weltanschauliche Briefe politischer Richtung, "*Schweizer Monatshefte,* XXXVI (1956), 189–93.
41. *Briefe, Neue erweiterte Ausgabe* (Frankfurt, 1959), pp. 466–68.

Chapter Ten

1. *The Novels of Hermann Hesse,* pp. 255–61.
2. On pp. 259–60, Ziolkowski alludes to the Kafkaesque aspect of the building in which the trial is held. The mystery and the bewilderment of the protagonist are suggestive of the trial of Joseph K. but the atmosphere lacks the *Angst,* the terror, that infuses Kafka's work, for here serenity prevails.
3. *The Journey to the East,* tr. Hilda Rosner. New York, 1957, p. 6.
4. Ziolkowski, *op. cit.,* p. 264.
5. *Ibid.,* p. 261.
6. Boulby, *op. cit.,* p. 257.
7. For a judicious critical evaluation, see E. R. Curtius, "Hermann Hesse," *Merkur,* I (1947), pp. 170 ff., and in *Kritische Essays zur europäischen Literatur,* pp. 202–23.
8. *Briefe. Erweiterte Ausgabe,* Frankfurt, 1964, p. 454.
9. E.g. from the chapter "Zwei Orden," published in *Corona* (1939) were deleted about one and a half pages (VI, 252–53), beginning: "Die grossen Männer. . . ." The passage refers to "corporals who from one day to the next become dictators."
10. *Briefe,* 1964, pp. 435–39.
11. See my article "On the Genesis of the *Glasperlenspiel,*" *The German Quarterly,* XLI (1968), 673–88.
12. For a more detailed comparison of changes between earlier and final versions, see *ibid.*
13. Ziolkowski, *The Novels of Hermann Hesse,* pp. 293–301.
14. *The German Quarterly,* XLI (1968), 683.
15. *Ibid.,* p. 674.
16. Johan Huizinga, *Homo Ludens: Vom Ursprung der Kultur im Spiel,* Rowohlt, Hamburg, 1956, p. 195. The philosophy of "play" may, of course, go back to Schiller's *Briefe über die ästhetische Erziehung des Menschen,* and the date of first publication of Huizinga's book (1938) precludes any influence on the introductory chapter of Hesse's novel. However, the book's theme formed the substance of Huizinga's inaugural lecture as rector of the University of Leyden in 1933. This lecture was given by Huizinga a few months later in Zürich and Vienna. Hesse was still in the habit of spending

part of the winter in Zürich or nearby Baden, so that he could easily have heard it himself, but, in any case, it was widely reported in the press.

17. In conversation with me, recorded in *Fünfter Archiv-Sonderdruck des westdeutschen Hermann Hesse-Archivs,* Cologne, 1957, pp. 8–9, 15.

18. *Die Entstehung des Doktor Faustus,* Amsterdam, 1949, p. 68.

19. *Hermann Hesse-Thomas Mann Briefwechsel,* Frankfurt, 1968, pp. 103–104.

20. For an amusing parody of the style of *Das Glasperlenspiel,* see Wolfgang Buhl, *Aepfel des Pegasus: Neue Parodien [Die Bank der Spötter,* Bd. 3], Berlin, 1953, pp. 51–52.

21. In view of Pasternak's life-long devotion to German literature —much of his life was spent translating it into Russian—it seems entirely possible that he knew Hesse's work and was influenced by it.

22. *Hesse—Mann Briefwechsel,* p. 103. With its overtones and ambiguities, this phrase is difficult to render, but the following version gives an approximation: "a nobly fatigued, sclerotically dignified omnium gatherum."

23. See Hesse's letter to Unseld who had queried discrepancies in style and perspectives: *G.S., VII,* 700–702.

24. Cf. Curt von Faber du Faur, "Zu Hermann Hesses *Glasperlenspiel,*" *Monatshefte,* XL (1948), 177–94.

25. E. R. Curtius, Review of Gide's *The Counterfeiters* in *Die Neue Rundschau,* XXXVII (1926), 655, discussed by Ziolkowski, *op. cit.,* pp. 224, 227.

26. Cf. especially Robert Musil, *Der Mann ohne Eigenschaften;* Ernst Jünger, *Heliopolis;* and Hermann Kasack, *Die Stadt hinter dem Strom.*

27. *Op. cit.,* p. 301.

28. It is possible that the name may allude to Ernst Bertram, the devoted follower or "shadow" of the poet Stefan George.

29. Letter of Hesse, VII, 702; cf. Burckhardt, *Weltgeschichtliche Betrachtungen,* esp. chs. 2, 4, 5.

30. Ziolkowski, *op. cit.,* pp. 315–16. If Burckhardt's influence goes a long way back, as Boulby claims, this observation tends to refute Ziolkowski's thesis of an original utopian intention.

31. Joseph Mileck, "Names and the Creative Process," *Monatshefte,* LIII (1961), 178, and *Herman Hesse and His Critics,* p. 188.

32. Inge D. Halpert, "The Alt-Musikmeister and Goethe," *Monatshefte,* LII (1960), 19–24.

33. J. C. Middleton, "An Enigma Transfigured," *German Life and Letters,* n.s., X (1956–1957), 302.

34. . Rudolf Koester, "Hesse's Music Master: In Search of a Prototype," *Forum for Modern Language Studies,* III (1967), 135–41.

Notes and References

35. In *Gespräche*, nr. 12 (Dec. 1962), mimeographed ·publication of thė *Freundesbund für Hermann Hesse* (Frankfurt).
36. *Briefe* (VII, 702).
37. *Op. cit.*, p. 286.
38. J. Jacobi, *The Psychology of C. G. Jung*, p. 145.
39. J. C. Middleton, "An Enigma Transfigured," *German Life and Letters*, n.s., X (1956–57), 298–302.
40. Boulby, *op. cit.*, pp. 290–91.
41. *G.S.*, VI, 556, the last stanza of Knecht's poem"Stufen": "Perhaps even the hour of death will confront us with new spaces; life's challenge to us will never end . . . very well then, heart, say farewell and recover new life!"
42. "Hermann Hesse im Banne Goethes: Bemerkungen zum *Glasperlenspiel*," *Revue des langues vivantes*, XXVI (1960), 432.
43. VI, 544: No being is granted us. We are only flux and we flow willingly into all forms: into day and night, cave and cathedral; we pass on through them, but we are driven by the thirst for being. . . . To become, once and for all, fixed in stone! At last to endure! Our longing is continually striving for that.
44. But perception of true life never died, and ours is the function and duty, through decay and destruction to preserve and continue the inspiration of sacred respect [for *Geist*], by means of symbol, simile, and song.
45. *Prosa aus dem Nachlass*, pp. 443–593.
46. Theodore Ziolkowski, "Hermann Hesse: Der vierte Lebenslauf," *Germanic Review*, XLII (1967), 124–43.
47. Mark Boulby, "The Fourth *Lebenslauf* as a Key to *Das Glasperlenspiel*," *Modern Language Review*, LXI (1966), 635–46.
48. Cf. my article "Music and Morality in Thomas Mann and Hermann Hesse," *University of Toronto Quarterly*, XXIV (1955), 175–90. Some of the following material is adapted from the article.
49. Letter to Otto Basler, August 25, 1934 (*G.S.*, VII, 571), repeated in part in *Das Glasperlenspiel* (VI, 100).
50. *Briefe*, Frankfurt, 1964, p. 457.

Chapter Eleven

1. "Préface au *Voyage en Orient* de Hermann Hesse," in *Préfaces* (Paris, 1948), p. 184.

Selected Bibliography

PRIMARY SOURCES

The major works are accessible in *Gesammelte Schriften,* 7 vols., Frankfurt: Suhrkamp, 1957. Most are also still available in regular Suhrkamp and, in some cases, in book club and paperback editions. Some of the more important items not found in the collected works are:

Hermann Hesse—Romain Rolland: Briefe. Zürich: Fretz and Wasmuth, 1954.

Briefe. Enl. edition. Frankfurt: Suhrkamp, 1964.

Prosa aus dem Nachlass, ed. Ninon Hesse. Frankfurt: Suhrkamp, 1965.

Kindheit und Jugend vor Neunzehnhundert: Hermann Hesse in Briefen und Lebenszeugnissen 1877–1895, ed. Ninon Hesse. Frankfurt: Suhrkamp, 1966.

Hermann Hesse—Thomas Mann: Briefwechsel, ed. Anni Carlsson, Frankfurt: Suhrkamp and Fischer, 1968.

Works of Hesse in English translation

Death and the Lover [*Narziss und Goldmund*], tr. Geoffrey Dunlop, New York: Dodd, Mead, 1932. Repr. under title *Goldmund* (London: Vision Press, 1959). Also translated by Ursule Molinaro under title *Narcissus and Goldmund.* (New York: Farrar, Straus and Giroux, 1968).

Demian, tr. N. H. Friday, repr. with foreword by Thomas Mann, New York: Holt, 1949. Tr. W. J. Strachan. (London: Vision Press, 1958. Also translated by Michael Roloff and Michael Lebeck, New York: Harper and Row, 1965).

Gertrude, tr. Hilda Rosner. London: Vision Press, 1955.

Selected Bibliography

The Journey to the East, tr. Hilda Rosner. New York: Noonday Press 1957. London: Vision Press, 1956.

Magister Ludi [*Das Glasperlenspiel*], tr. Mervyn Savill. New York: Holt, 1949. Repr. New York: Ungar, 1957.

Peter Camenzind, tr. W. J. Strachan. London: Vision Press, 1961.

The Prodigy [*Unterm Rad*], tr. W. J. Strachan. London: Vision Press, 1958. Also translated by Michael Roloff and Michael Lebeck under title *Beneath the Wheel.* (New York: Farrar, Straus and Giroux, 1968).

Siddhartha, tr. Hilda Rosner. New York: New Directions, 1957. London: Vision Press, 1954.

Steppenwolf, tr. by Basil Creighton, revised by Walter Sorell. New York: Random House, 1963. Tr. revised by Joseph Mileck and Horst Frenz. (New York: Holt, Rinehart and Winston, 1963).

SECONDARY SOURCES

(a) Bibliographies:

BAREISS, OTTO. *Hermann Hesse. Eine Bibliographie der Werke über Hermann Hesse.* Basel: Karl Maier-Bader, vol. I, 1962; vol. II, 1964.

MILECK, JOSEPH. *Hermann Hesse and his Critics.* Chapel Hill: Univ. of North Carolina Press, 1958.

WAIBLER, HELMUT. *Hermann Hesse. Eine Bibliographie.* Berne, Munich: Francke, 1962.

(b) In German:

BALL, HUGO. *Hermann Hesse. Sein Leben und sein Werk.* New ed. cont. by Anni Carlsson and Otto Basler. Zürich: Fretz and Wasmuth, 1947. Still the best biography in German with excellent added chapters on the late works.

BAUMER, FRANZ. *Hermann Hesse* [*Köpfe des 20.Jahrhunderts,* 10]. Berlin: Colloquium, 1959. Good introduction for the German reader.

BOECKMANN, PAUL. "Hermann Hesse," in *Deutsche Literatur im 20.Jahrhundert.* Heidelberg: Rothe, 1954.

BUBER, MARTIN. "Hermann Hesses Dienst am Geist," *Neue deutsche Hefte,* IV (1957–8), 387–93.

CAST, G. C. "Hermann Hesse als Erzieher," *Monatshefte,* XLIII (1951), 207–20.

CURTIUS, ERNST ROBERT. "Hermann Hesse," in *Kritische Essays zur europäischen Literatur.* Berne: Francke, 1950.

DAHRENDORF, MALTE. "Hermann Hesses *Demian* und C. G. Jung," *Germanisch-Romanische Monatsschrift*, XXXIX (1958), 81–97.

DERMINE, RENE. "Hermann Hesse im Banne Goethes: Bemerkungen zum *Glasperlenspiel*," *Revue des Langues Vivantes*, XXVI (1960), 430–36.

DUERR, WERNER. *Hermann Hesse: Vom Wesen der Musik in der Dichtung*. Stuttgart: Silberburg, 1957.

FABER DU FAUR, CURT VON. "Zu Hermann Hesses *Glasperlenspiel*," *Monatshefte*, XL (1948), 177–94.

GRENZMANN, WILHELM. "Hermann Hesse: Geist und Sinnlichkeit," in *Dichtung und Glaube*. Bonn: Athenäum, 1964.

HILL, CLAUDE. "Hermann Hesse als Kritiker der bürgerlichen Zivilisation," *Monatshefte*, XL (1948), 241–53.

HIRSCHBACH, FRANK D. "Traum und Vision bei Hermann Hesse," *Monatshefte*, LI (1959), 157–68.

KASACK, HERMANN. "Hermann Hesse" in *Mosaiksteine*. Frankfurt: Suhrkamp, 1956.

KILCHENMANN, RUTH. "Hermann Hesse und die Dinge," *German Quarterly*, XXX (1957), 238–46.

KOHLSCHMIDT, WERNER. "Meditationen über Hermann Hesses *Glasperlenspiel*," *Zeitwende*, XIX (1947–8), 154–70.

MATZIG, RICHARD B. *Hermann Hesse: Studien zu Werk und Innenwelt des Dichters*. Stuttgart: Reclam, 1949.

MAYER, GERHART. "Hermann Hesse: Mystische Religiosität und dichterische Form," *Jahrbuch der deutschen Schillergesellschaft*, IV (1960), 434–62.

MAYER, HANS. "Hermann Hesse und das 'Feuilletonistische Zeitalter,'" in *Studien zur deutschen Literatur*. Berlin: Rütten & Loening, 1955.

————. "Hesses *Glasperlenspiel* oder die Wiederbegegnung," in *Ansichten. Zur Literatur der Zeit*. Reinbek bei Hamburg: Rowohlt, 1962.

PANNWITZ, RUDOLF. *Hermann Hesses west-östliche Dichtung*. Frankfurt: Suhrkamp, 1957.

PUPPE, HEINZ W. "Psychologie und Mystik in 'Klein und Wagner' von Hermann Hesse," *PMLA*, LXXVIII (1963), pp. 28–35.

SCHMID, MAX. *Hermann Hesse: Weg und Wandlung*. Zürich: Fretz and Wasmuth, 1947.

SCHWARTZ, EGON. "Zur Erklärung von Hesses *Steppenwolf*," *Monatshefte*, LIII (1961), 191–98.

SEIDLIN, OSKAR. "H. Hesses *Glasperlenspiel*," *Germanic Review*, XXIII (1948), 263–73.

STRICH, FRITZ. "Dank an Hermann Hesse" in *Der Dichter und die Zeit*. Berne: Francke, 1947.

Selected Bibliography

ZELLER, BERNHARD. *Hermann Hesse. Eine Chronik in Bildern.* Frankfurt: Suhrkamp, 1960. Excellent photographs of scenes from Hesse's life and work.

————. *Hermann Hesse in Selbstzeugnissen und Bilddokumenten.* Reinbek bei Hamburg: Rowohlt, 1963. Excellent pictures and commentary.

(c) In French:

COLLEVILLE, MAURICE. "Le problème religieux dans la vie et dans l'oeuvre de Hermann Hesse, *"Etudes germaniques,* VII (1952), 123–48; VIII (1953), 182.

DEBRUGE, SUZANNE. "L'oeuvre de Hermann Hesse et la psychanalyse," *Etudes germaniques,* VII (1952), 252–61.

(d) In English:

ANDREWS, R. C. "The Poetry of Hermann Hesse," *German Life and Letters,* VI (1952–53), 117–27.

BENN, MAURICE. "An Interpretation of the Work of Hermann Hesse," *German Life and Letters,* III (1949–50), 202–11.

BOULBY, MARK. *Hermann Hesse: His Mind and Art.* Ithaca: Cornell U. P., 1967. The best full-length study in depth and detail.

————. "The Fourth 'Lebenslauf' as a Key to *Das Glasperlenspiel,*" *Modern Language Review,* LXI (1966), 635–46.

COHN, HILDE D. "The Symbolic End of Hermann Hesse's *Glasperlenspiel.*" *Modern Language Quarterly,* XI (1950), 347–57.

COLBY, THOMAS E. "The Impenitent Prodigal: Hermann Hesse's Hero," *The German Quarterly,* XL (1967), 14–23.

ENGEL, EVA J. "Hermann Hesse," in *German Men of Letters,* vol. II, London: Wolff, 1963, 249–74. An introductory essay.

FARQUHARSON, ROBERT H. "The Identity and Significance of Leo in Hesse's *Morgenlandfahrt,*" *Monatshefte,* LV (1963), 122–28.

FICKERT, KURT J. "The Development of the Outsider Concept in Hesse's Novels," *Monatshefte,* LII (1960), 171–78.

FIELD, G. W. "Music and Morality in Thomas Mann and Hermann Hesse," *Univ. of Toronto Quarterly,* XXIV (1955), 175–90.

————. "Hermann Hesse: A Neglected Nobel Prize Novelist," *Queen's Quarterly,* LXV (1958), 514–20.

————. "Hermann Hesse as Critic of English and American Literature," *Monatshefte,* LIII (1961), 147–58.

————. "On the Genesis of Hesse's *Glasperlenspiel,*" *The German Quarterly,* XLI (1968), 673–88.

FREEDMAN, RALPH. *The Lyrical Novel: Studies in Hermann Hesse, André Gide and Virginia Woolf.* Princeton, U. P. 1963. Interesting in its comparative perspective, not always reliable in details of interpretation of Hesse.

GOLDGAR, HARRY. "Hesse's Glasperlenspiel and the Game of Go," *German Life and Letters*, XX (1966), 132–37.

GONTRUM, PETER B. "Hermann Hesse as a Critic of French Literature," *Symposium*, XIX (1965), 226–35.

HALLAMORE, JOYCE. "Paul Klee, H. H. and *Die Morgenlandfahrt*," *Seminar*, I (1965), 17–24.

HALPERT, INGE D. "The Alt-Musikmeister and Goethe," *Monatshefte*, LII (1960), 19–24.

————. "Vita activa and vita contemplativa," *Monatshefte*, LIII (1961), 159–66.

HELLER, PETER. "The Writer in Conflict with his Age: A Study in the Ideology of Hermann Hesse," *Monatshefte*, XLVI (1954), 137–47.

————. "The Creative Unconscious and the Spirit: A Study of Polarities in Hesse's Image of the Writer," *Modern Language Forum*, XXXVIII (1953), 28–40.

JOHNSON, SIDNEY M. "The Autobiographies in Hermann Hesse's *Glasperlenspiel*," *German Quarterly*, XXIX (1956), 160–171.

KOESTER, RUDOLF. "The Portrayal of Age in Hesse's Narrative Prose," *Germanic Review*, XLI (1966), 111–19.

————. "Hesse's Music Master: In Search of a Prototype," *Forum for Modern Language Studies*, III (1967), 135–41.

————. "Self-Realization: Hesse's Reflections on Youth," *Monatshefte*, LVII (1965), 181–86.

MAURER, WARREN R. "Jean Paul and Hermann Hesse: *Katzenberger* and *Kurgast*," *Seminar*, IV (1968), 113–28.

MIDDLETON, J. C., "Hermann Hesse's *Morgenlandfahrt*," *Germanic Review*, XXXII (1957), 299–310.

————. "An Enigma Transfigured in Hermann Hesse's *Glasperlenspiel*," *German Life and Letters*, n.s. X (1956-57), 298–302.

MIHAILOVICH, VASA D. "Hermann Hesse as a Critic of Russian Literature," *Arcadia*, II (1967), 91–102.

MILECK, JOSEPH. "The Poetry of Hermann Hesse," *Monatshefte*, LXVI (1954), 192–98.

————. "The Prose of Hermann Hesse: Life, Substance and Form," *The German Quarterly*, XXVII (1954), 163–74.

————. "Names and the Creative Process," *Monatshefte*, LIII (1961), 167–80.

NAUMANN, WALTER. "The Individual and Society in the Work of Hermann Hesse," *Monatshefte*, XLI (1949), 33–42.

NEGUS, KENNETH. "On the Death of Joseph Knecht in Hermann Hesse's *Glasperlenspiel*," *Monatshefte*, LIII (1961), 181–89.

Selected Bibliography

NORTON, ROGER C. "Variant Endings of Hesse's *Glasperlenspiel,*" *Monatshefte,* LX (1968), 141–46.

ROSE, ERNST. *Faith from the Abyss. Hermann Hesse's Way from Romanticism to Modernity.* New York: Columbia, 1965.

SEIDLIN, OSKAR. "H. Hesse's *Glasperlenspiel,*" *Germanic Review,* XXIII (1948), 263–73.

_____. "Hermann Hesse. The Exorcism of the Demon," *Symposium,* IV (1950), 325–48. Repr. *Essays in German and Comparative Literature.* Chapel Hill, 1961, pp. 203–27.

SHAW, LEROY R. "Time and the Structure of Hermann Hesse's *Siddhartha,*" *Symposium,* XI (1957), 204–24.

ZIOLKOWSKI, THEODORE. *The Novels of Hermann Hesse: A Study in Theme and Structure.* Princeton, U. P. 1965. The best full-length study of the major works in breadth and perspective.

_____. "Hermann Hesse's Chiliastic Vision," *Monatshefte,* LIII (1961), 199–210.

_____. "Hermann Hesse: Der vierte Lebenslauf," *Germanic Review,* XLII (1967), 124–43.

_____. *Hermann Hesse,* New York [Columbia Essays on Modern Writers, no. 22], 1966. This pamphlet gives a good introductory sketch.

ADDENDUM:

Since this book was set in print a new and better translation of *Das Glasperlenspiel* by Richard and Clara Winston under the title *The Glass Bead Game* has been published by Holt, Rinehart and Winston (New York, 1969).

Index

Index

Woltereck, Richard, 73

Zeller, Bernhard, 35, 137, 175n, 184n
Ziolkowski, Theodore, vii, 46, 58, 59,

84, 92, 103, 104, 105, 107, 111, 143,
145, 152, 176n, 177n, 180n, 185n,
186n, 187n
Zoroaster, 53, 144